Creation and Cosmology

Creation and Cosmology

Attempt at Sketching a Modern Christian Theology of Nature

A Collection of Essays Contributing to the Discussion Between Christianity and Modern Science.

Rudolf B. Brun

To order additional copies of this book, contact:
Xlibris Corporation
1-888-795-4274
www.Xlibris.com
Orders@Xlibris.com
51737

CONTENTS

FOR THE CHURCH
And in memory of my teachers:
Adolf Portmann,
Gustav Siewerth, and
Hans Urs Cardinal von Balthasar.

INTRODUCTION

This little book contains a collection of essays that, except one, were published either in *Zygon: Journal of Religion and Science* or in *Communio: International Catholic Review*. The reason to publish them again is to make these writings available to a wider public. I hope that these articles may especially reach those Christians struggling with the difficult task of trying to integrate the major insights of modern science into a Christian understanding of creation. I also hope that the content of these essays may further stimulate discussions among the authorities of the church. The task to update the Christian theology of nature is urgent. This is because the Christian message, including its understanding of creation, needs to be rejuvenated for our time; the credibility of the church is at stake.

The publications all deal with the difficult topic of science and religion or, more precisely, with general, cosmic evolution and Christianity. The topic is difficult because there is no obvious connection between a worldview from modern science and Christian faith. This situation often leads to schizophrenia-like situations in people that strive to follow Christian teachings and are well informed about the discoveries of modern science. For example, biblical teachings about the origin of creation, and our place within it, clash with the views from science. The discovery that our universe came about through its own history, not by supernatural intervention(s), does not easily harmonize with Christian tradition. Yet theology cannot simply let go of the basic message in the biblical story of creation. Its central message is that the word of God creates creation. The major problem therefore is: How can we reconcile the revelation that the word of God creates creation with the view from science that nature is capable of bringing forth itself? [For an attempt see below, and the essays: "Integrating Evolution: A Contribution to the Christian Doctrine of Creation (*Zygon*, vol. 29, no. 3 [September 1994]) and "Can

God Be God in That Which Is Not God? Attempt at a Christology-Centered View of Creation" (Communio, submitted)].

Granted, if the story of creation would be told today, it would be quite different from what the authors of Genesis wrote about some three thousand years ago. Science has made tremendous progress in uncovering how our world really came into existence, not in seven days but in fourteen billion years! A tremendously mighty explosion, an unimaginable powerful event, far beyond any human conception or understanding, released the energy out of which the entire universe emerged overtime. However, this result, a stupendous achievement of modern physics, does not provide us with a detailed insight into what happened in this instant. Yet, physicists found out what happened within minutes after the original explosion. Yet as they try to move closer and closer toward an understanding of that, first instant from which time and space emerged, the physics, as we know it, breaks down. What we do know, however, is that within the blink of an eye, the first particles froze out of the tremendous energy released in the big bang. These primordial "particles" were the carriers of the emerging laws of nature. The laws of nature emerged from the sequence in which these first force-carrying particle(s) split and differentiated. Through this differentiation process, gravity, electromagnetism, and the strong and the weak forces came into existence (the latter two organize the cohesion and radiation of atomic components).

In spite of these amazing discoveries, there are still tremendous gaps in our knowledge. One of these is the rather painful realization that we can only detect about four percent of the structures of the universe. The vast majority of its architecture, about eighty two percent, does not radiate and therefore is dark for our instruments. Another deep problem at this time is why the expansion of the universe seems to be accelerating. There are hints that space itself is increasing ever faster and, in this way, driving the billions of stars and galaxies farther apart from one another. If the universe is indeed expanding faster and faster, then there must be an unknown, tremendous force throughout the universe that is driving this expansion. At present, we have no clue what this dark energy may be.

What we do know, however, is that from the original explosion of the big bang to our time, the complexity within our universe has increased tremendously. It increased from the first atoms that crystallized from the original soup of energy and quarks to the first atoms. From these, increasingly complex atoms were, and still are, synthesized in the center of the stars. The energy produced in their atomic furnaces prevents the stars from collapsing under their own weight. If the nuclear fuel runs out, however, stars collapse under their own gravity, caving into themselves. The heat caused by the friction of the collapsing matter might become so intense that stars explode as supernovae. Such events generate interstellar dust clouds from which planetary systems may form. In this way, the planets inherit the complex materials that were synthesized in the generation of the stars that preceded the ripping apart of the exploding star. Countless planetary systems formed this way, including our solar system. This is how the Earth came into existence. As it formed some four billion years ago it became endowed with the atomic and molecular building blocks that had formed in the generations of stars that preceded the supernova explosion.

From these inherited materials, further complexification by chemical syntheses continued on the primordial Earth. Complexification is a result of sequential syntheses, and syntheses bring forth novelties. This is, however, not only the case in chemistry but is also the central creative phenomenon that brought forth the entire universe.

Synthesis, the unification of elements, brings forth new structures. Synthesis brings forth entities with qualities totally different from the qualities of the elements from which the novelty was synthesized. This is the phenomenon of emergence, the central phenomenon of the creativity of nature.

Synthesis, however, depends on the availability of energy. The energy that drives the natural creative process of sequential syntheses ultimately originated in the original explosion of the big bang. All of that we call matter, all the innumerable galaxies and stars ultimately froze out of this primordial energy.

On the just-forming Earth, there was plenty of energy available. One source was the radiation of abundant radioactive elements. Energy also came from the heat generated by the impacts of asteroids that slammed into the young Earth, and of course, the radiation from the sun provided still another source of energy. Therefore, there was plenty of energy available to drive chemical complexification.

The chemical sequence of synthetic steps that led to the emergence of life to day is still unknown. This gap in our knowledge, however, cannot be "bridged" by arguing that the appearance of life was the result of supernatural intervention. After all the lessons religion had to painfully learn from the history of science, it would be foolish indeed to again argue for a God of the gaps! Eventually, scientists will find out how life emerged from pre-life entities.

Once life evolved from the synthesis of pre-life molecules, the capacity to multiply emerged. One important condition for this to happen is the presence of information-carrying molecules. How these molecules formed is still unclear, but they must have been the templates from which it became possible to construct new life from already existing life.

Once the first organisms emerged, evolution became unavoidable. Why? Because a cohort of replicating entities must compete for the available energy and resources in order to multiply. Due to variation in the transmission of the information-carrying templates from one generation to the next, the individuals of a population of organisms are not identical. Some individuals will be slightly more efficient to produce offspring than others. Overtime, the faster-multiplying organisms will replace the less prolific ones. As this happens, the conditions in the environment will change. It will change because a growing population, by the mere fact of expanding, will increase the competition between the individuals. In addition, the climate may also change and with it many parameters influencing survival, including the quality and quantity of available nutrients.

As a population of organisms expands, groups of individuals may become separated from the original cohort. Geographical barriers such as streams, valleys, or mountain chains may prevent mating between the new and the old populations. Overtime, the isolated population may evolve in different directions than the original group. Such events, and other population-isolating forces, lead to the evolution of new species. This is Darwinism! It is evolution through the creative two-step process of variation and natural selection.

Darwin was very much puzzled by the phenomenon of variation; how to explain it lead to speculations along Lamarckian hypotheses. Lamarck's basic idea was that advantages acquired in the lifetime of the parents could be passed on to their offspring. In this view, gradual progressive adaptation of organisms in evolution was due to the capacity of the parents to pass on acquired skills to their offspring. This was the Lamarckian explanation why organisms were so well adapted to their environment. Genetics, however, disproved the possibility of such a mechanism. The discovery was that the genes, involved in the construction of the body, were totally separated from the genes that are passed on to the new generations. There is no sharing of genes between those that construct the body of an organism and the genes involve in directing the formation of eggs and sperms.

That genes could mutate was the crucial discovery. It explained why there were variations between organisms even of the same species; spontaneous changes in the genetic material could generate new traits. In the fruit fly, for example, white eyes could appear suddenly instead of the normally present red eyes.

One important aspect of this discovery was, and still is, that the occurrence of mutations is unpredictable, at least for individual cases. It is unpredictable because the frequency of mutations follows the laws of probability. Consequently, mutation rates can only be predicted statistically. For example, in rapidly multiplying organisms such as bacteria the frequency of a particular mutation to occur is roughly one in one hundred million. Mutations, however, are not only happening in fast-proliferating organisms. They occur in all organisms, although in ways less obvious because animals and plants reproduce much more slowly than bacteria. Farmers and breeders learnt thousands of years ago to take advantage of this fact by selecting favorable mutations. This made it possible to domesticate plants and animals, such as corn, wheat, goats, and cows.

Variations, however, are not just the consequence of spontaneously changing genetic information as neo-Darwinism suggested some decades ago. Variation occurs also because of differences in how genetic information is used. The utterly surprising finding these days is that vastly different organisms may have quite similar genes. Vast differences in body plans and architectures are not primarily a result of the different qualities and quantities of genes but how old genes are regulated in new ways. This is to say that genes that were assembled hundreds of millions of years ago in bacteria and molds are still part of modern forms of life, worms, flies, mice, rats, and primates, including us!

The reason to point this out in the context of the essays in this booklet is to emphasize the fact that we human beings are a part of the evolutionary history of life. We emerged from within this history in similar ways all other organisms came into existence. All forms of life that ever existed, or still roam the Earth, have ancestors from whom they descended overtime through variation and natural selection.

At the level of life, evolution works in this way. However, there was, and still is, evolution long before there were organisms. Yet in the physical universe, evolution works not through variations in populations, variations that natural selection my favor, but evolution, as I have briefly outlined above, is the result of syntheses. Do we not have to assume that at the level of life syntheses may play a similarly important role in bringing forth new organisms? Does organismic evolution perhaps also work by bringing forth new genomes by syntheses of old genetic programs into new genomes? How this fundamental creative process may work to bring forth new organisms is a matter of current research. What is already certain, however, is that we humans carry old genetic programs in our genome. It was synthesized by nature from old genetic programs. Elements that already existed were integrated in new ways. We too are a product of the creativity of nature. It universally brings forth the new through synthesis of the old. Like everything else, the stars, the galaxies, the sun, the moon, the grass, the flowers of the fields, and all that lives in the sea, on land, and in the air, all this wonderful diversity is the outcome of emergence through synthesis. Yes, we have a special place within all these wonders! It is the place from which we are able to investigate, recognize, and appreciate the majestic spectacle of creation.

Because we are an outcome of nature, nature brought forth our creative and reflective mind. Reflecting over the tremendous, wonderful world a basic question may emerge in our mind: What is the source of the creativity of nature? What is the center of nature from which all its creative power springs forth? To put this question into philosophical terms: *What is the nature of nature?*

This collection of essays attempts to give an answer to this question. Because of my personal life history, the people I met, the teachers that influenced me, the answer to this central question comes from within Christianity. At its center, so I learnt from Hans Urs Cardinal von Balthasar, is the revelation that God is love. If this is so, and I believe it is, then creation is the gift of the loving God. The gift of God to that, which is *essentially* not God; the gift from the one *who is,* to that *which is not.* Christianity refers to this act of creation as *creatio ex nihilo* (creation out of nothing). What can Christianity say about the nature of this gift? The gift is the Word of God. It is the Word of God out of which all of creation becomes. This gift of God to creation is His Word, truly given away. Through this act of giving, the Word of God belongs to creation. Thanks to this gift creation receives the power to become itself.

What is the nature of this Word that God gives away to creation? The nature of God's Word is God himself! For "in the beginning was the Word, and the Word was with God, and the Word was God" (John 1:1-2).

If the Word of God *that is God* is the gift of God through which creation receives the power to become itself, how can the Word of God that *is* God become that *which is not God?* We Christians celebrate Christmas every year. We celebrate that the Word of God, the Son of God, became one of us. We celebrate the mystery of incarnation, the mystery that God can become that which is not God but a human being. At Christmastime, therefore, we should celebrate not only the birth of Christ but also the birth of creation. This is because there is only one root to both: God's logic of incarnation!

For "the mystery of the Incarnation will always remain the central point of reference for an understanding of the enigma of human existence, the created world and God himself. The challenge of this mystery pushes philosophy to its limits, as reason is summoned to make its own a logic, which brings down the walls within which it risks being confined.[1] Why is there incarnation? Why did God make this gift of His Word to nothingness so that creation may become? Why did the Father give His Son away so that creation not only may become but also be saved? He did all that because God is love (*Deus caritas est*)![2]

---

[1]   Pope John Paul II, letter to the Bishops of the Catholic Church, 1998, # 84.
[2]   *God is love.* First encyclical of Pope Benedict XVI on 25. December 2005.

INTEGRATING EVOLUTION: A CONTRIBUTION TO THE CHRISTIAN DOCTRINE OF CREATION

Zygon, vol. 29, no. 3 [September 1994])

Abstract. Science has demonstrated that the universe creates itself through its own history. This history is the result of a probabilistic process, not a deterministic execution of a plan. Science has also documented that human beings are a result of this universal, probabilistic process of general evolution. At first sight, these results seem to contradict Christian teaching. According to the Bible, history is essentially the history of salvation. Human beings therefore are not an "accident of nature" but special creations to be saved. With deeper theological probing, it becomes clearer, however, that creation must create itself. The Christian God is the loving God who enters into a loving relationship with human beings if they desire to reciprocate. If creation could not create itself, human beings could not be free. Without freedom to ignore or reject God's love, the central act of the Christian God, the drama of salvation, would become a parody played by marionettes in the hands of a supernatural manipulator. Christians should welcome the fundamental insight brought forth by science that the universe, including human beings, created itself through its own history. This article will try to show that this scientific insistence is required and confirmed by the intrinsic character of the Orthodox, Judeo-Christian concept of God. That nature has to create itself, including human beings, secures human freedom and, with it, the responsibility for human actions. From this perspective, one might better understand the Bible in the light of God's revelation through the book of nature.

The goal of this article is to suggest a way toward integrating evolution into an updated Christian doctrine of creation. The point of departure for this attempt will be Hegel's reflection on the Christian doctrine of the Trinitarian God. This reflection of the nature of God as "otherness" within God (Trinity) and "otherness" outside of God (nature) might provide the foundation for securing the relationship between the loving Christian God and God's creation.

For Hegel, the end point of creation, its purpose, is given from the beginning. This goal is the unification of God and creation in the God-man Jesus Christ. The sequential transformations from the physical universe to life and from there through higher and higher organisms are understood as steps of the ascending spirit. The spirit begins alienated from itself and moves toward becoming itself. Hegel understands cosmogenesis as sequential transformations of the spirit from lower into higher forms of life. Finally, the spirit finds itself at the level of the human mind because at this level, the spirit is capable of finding itself through reflecting on itself. For Hegel, it is the rising spirit that drives creation toward increased perfection. Hegel carefully studied the results that science produced in his time. His view found support in the work of Jean-Baptist Lamarck. In Lamarck's view, as well as in Hegel's philosophical system of nature, evolution was caused by a trend toward increased perfection.

The Hegel-Lamarckian position became undermined by Charles Darwin's discovery of the interplay between organismic variation and natural selection. The discovery of this mechanism of evolution explained how nature could evolve by natural law without any goal-oriented process toward increasing perfection.

Since Darwin's discovery of this natural driving force of evolution, the neo-Darwinian understanding of evolution as the result of the interplay between genetic variation (mutations) and natural selection has found overwhelming confirmation. Why then even bring up Hegel's old-fashioned view on cosmogenesis? It is because his theological point of departure, Hegel's understanding of nature as "otherness of God outside of God" (nothingness), is the Christian insight into the nature of creation as creation out of nothing *(creatio ex nihilo)*. The theological point of departure for Hegel's cosmology, therefore, is at the center of the Christian doctrine of creation. But what about the scientific dimension of Hegel's view? First and foremost, modern science has to reject the notion that cosmogenesis has a purpose, that it is goal oriented toward the formation of human beings, for example. The fundamental reason for this rejection is the insight that cosmogenesis, including the emergence of human beings, is the result of a historical process. Universal evolution is essentially a probabilistic, not a deterministic process. It is what actually happens among possible events that create history. Any form of cosmic teleology negates genuine cosmic history. Teleology holds that what actually happens is the execution of a plan, or what boils down to the same distortion, there is purpose in "history" because there is a goal to reach. Modern cosmology has made it abundantly clear that evolution is not a deterministic realization of a plan already given at the start. Nature is not like a train heading toward a predetermined destination. Rather, nature has the creative power to create itself through its own history. Part of this history is the emergence of human beings from the natural process. Science, therefore, has found that human beings are the result of the natural process of evolution capable of creating itself.

This is crucial because becoming itself through history is also the basis for human beings to become themselves! This freedom of human beings, this essential empowerment to become themselves through freedom of choice, fits the essence of the Christian message precisely: without freedom, the relationship between God and humans cannot make sense. It cannot make sense because without freedom, there cannot be love. Determinism by God contradicts the free reciprocity that characterizes the Christian theological understanding of love.

For this reason, the Russian philosopher and theologian Vladimir Solovyev (1851-1900) welcomed Darwin's discovery that organismic evolution was driven by the natural process of variation and selection. Solovyev saw the importance of nature creating itself. The way from Lamarck to Darwin led Solovyev to understand nature to be on the way toward freedom. Evolution is the safeguard of human freedom, the freedom to enter into a genuine relationship with the Creator. Solovyev's view of nature underscores the importance of natural evolution as a self-creating, historic process that brings the essence of the Christian message into the center of creation.

Finally, I will try to integrate the insight that evolution does not execute a plan with the Christian message that God has a plan for His creation, namely, to save it.

I. COSMOGENESIS

The Evolution of Matter. Over the last fifty years or so, scientists discovered that evolution, first documented in the organismic world, was also the fundamental process by which the inorganic world emerged. Nuclear physicists as well as astrophysicists succeeded in describing the origin of matter from the original big bang in surprising detail (Weinberg 1977).[1] The basic mechanism driving this evolution is the synthesis of previously synthesized

elements into new entities under appropriate environmental conditions
(Fowler 1984, 922).[2] The bottom line is that synthesis brings forth novelty.

Chemical Evolution. The synthesis of molecules into compounds with
new properties is the domain of chemistry. New substances emerge from the
synthesis of elements under appropriate conditions. During the evolution of
the universe, including the solar system with the early Earth, extensive chemical
evolution took place. Increasingly complex molecules were synthesized, thanks
to the availability of energy and suitable chemical environments. The new
molecules generated new chemical niches. In some of these, the conditions
became appropriate by chance, thereby providing new chemical environments
in which more complex compounds could emerge.[3]

A central aspect of evolution at all levels of organization is that complexity
of systems can increase as long as there is energy flowing into such systems.
Systems that are capable of taking up matter or energy are open systems
capable of forming spontaneous patterns. There is plenty of energy from the
original big bang, for example, in the materials and radiations of the stars,
including our sun, to drive morphogenesis in such open systems. There are
mathematically defined states in which such systems are stable (Prigogine
1980, 89, 106, 128; Brooks and Wiley 1986, 77).

A given dynamical system might take up matter or energy to the point of
instability. If there is enough energy available, the system will "jump" from its
prior stage to a new stable state. The generation of new atoms from old ones
as well as the synthesis of new chemical compounds from simpler molecules
are examples of such morphogenetic events.

Biological Evolution.   Chemistry demonstrates that the generation
of new molecules by synthesis from already synthesized ones is practically
without limits. The chemical processes that occurred during the history of our
planet led to the formation of increasingly complex compounds, ultimately
resulting in the synthesis of self-replicating molecules (see Engel, Macko, and
Silfer 1990, 47; Hanawalt 1980; Graham 1972, 257). These self-replicating
molecules, most likely RNA,[4] probably became encapsulated into vesicles.
Bilayered vesicles (micelles) that can catalyze their own replication were
recently described (Bachmann et al. 1992; see also Cairns-Smith 1982). The
details of how life originated need to be worked out, but there can be no
doubt that life emerged as a result of general evolution. Very likely, a multistep
process produced cells by integrating other organic entities (Margulis 1984,
75). The appearance of life was again a qualitative jump analogous to those

resulting from the synthesis of subatomic particles into atoms or the synthesis of atoms into molecules.

Organismic evolution continued with the aggregation of cells. The cells in such aggregates were most likely capable of executing all living functions, but in a colony, this was no longer necessary. The cells on the outside, for example, were able to save energy by turning off the "inside" functions and vice versa. Task sharing, or differentiation, in such aggregates probably happened by suppression of specific functions. This resulted in increased energy efficiency and provided regeneration capacities to the aggregates. For example, if "outside" cells were lost, "inside" cells were capable of replacing them by turning on previously dormant "outside" functions.

In a next synthetic step, the cellular aggregates associated with one another. This created primitive organisms consisting of a series of identical segments. Originally, each segment was probably again capable of executing all of the functions necessary for its survival as a unit. By associating with one another, the segments were again able to save energy by turning off functions. For example, those segments located anteriorly did not need to express posterior functions anymore. In this way, perhaps anteroposterior polarization of such wormlike organisms might have occurred. Because this synthetic arrangement improved energy efficiency, the population could increase in number. This in turn made it possible for these creatures to expand into new habitats.

It is important to see that the synthetic event, namely, increased energy efficiency in this case obtained through aggregation, happened first. Only after this event were these organisms capable of increasing their number. The point is that an endogenous synthetic event has to happen before natural selection can enter into action. The creative event occurs endogenously and emerges from within the already existing system. Natural selection then may (or may not) act upon the new invention, fine-tuning adaptation by favoring efficient reproduction. To acknowledge the central importance of emergence for evolution does not introduce any vitalistic or supernatural force into evolution. "Emergentism is a thoroughly materialistic philosophy" (Mayr 1982, 63).[5] Throughout evolution, the emergence of novelty, invention, takes priority over natural selection.[6]

Since the beginning of the twentieth century, it has become increasingly clear that mutations, spontaneous changes in the genome, are the basis of inheritable organismic variations. It is also evident that mutations occur with certain frequencies. Mutation rates depend on many factors. There are exogenous factors, such as mutagenic chemicals, irradiation, and perhaps viruses. There are also endogenous factors, such as spontaneous mutations related to the chemistry and the internal organization of the genetic material (DNA). The evolution of higher organisms from lower forms of life depended on genetic change. Could the genome be subjected to integrative, synthetic processes analogous to the ones discussed so far? If this were indeed the case, multiplying first identical genes would have formed genetic aggregates. In such gene clusters, one functional gene would have been sufficient to maintain the original function. The rest of the genes in the cluster could mutate without jeopardizing necessary gene functions. The result of these mutations in redundant genes would have been the generation of genetic diversity within an originally identical gene cluster: a family of genes might have formed (Ohno 1970, 32; Raff and Raff 1985, 203). In a changing environment, for example, of fluctuating water temperatures or varying water salinity, a gene within that family but different from the original one might have functioned more efficiently than the gene from which it originated. This genetic variation caused by mutations helped the organism to survive in a new environment. The individuals that had these genes had a selective advantage over the ones that did not possess them. The synthetic process operating at the genetic level would have continued by producing identical gene families. These families subsequently diversified by various types of mutations, and in a third step, their new functions became integrated into the genome.

Integration of diversity leads to the emergence of novelty. In the case of organisms, integration of genetic diversity leads to the formation of new genetic units (genotypes). Such new genomes will allow the formation of new organisms (phenotypes). Obviously, these creatures will only be able to survive if they occupy a niche in which they are able to reproduce in sufficient numbers. Again, natural selection is a crucial but secondary factor. The primary event is innovation. Innovation is the fundamental phenomenon of cosmogenesis. In physical as well as organismic evolution, it is synthesis that creates novelty. Mutations are of crucial importance in organismic evolution, but they happen in the context of a genome that already exists. A new mutation may not have a crucial effect on an organism because a genetic change happened but because that change occurred in the context of an already existing genetic network. To say that mutations and selection cause speciation is reductionist language because the importance of the genetic context in which mutations have their effects is ignored.[7] This is why I have difficulties with the formula "mutation and selection" for organismic evolution. This neo-Darwinian explanation overemphasizes the importance of natural selection and fails to recognize the phenomenon of emergence. This is why it cannot provide any insight into the physical evolution of the universe: where there is no reproduction, Darwinian natural selection cannot work, yet there is still evolution. Emergence is the spontaneous appearance of novelty through an event integrating already existing elements into novelty. Emergence occurs in physical as well as in organismic evolution.

In organismic evolution, genes are the "already existing elements" that may form new genomes through integrative events. One reason why most biologists claim that the neo-Darwinian model of evolution is sufficient to explain speciation is that embryology, developmental genetics, has not yet been integrated into "the modern synthesis." Neo-Darwinism is too heavily dependent upon data collected from populations of adult organisms. Adults cannot form new species: birds did not evolve from adult dinosaurs. Rather, the developmental programs that drive embryogenesis must have changed. Over the last ten years or so, developmental genetics has made splendid progress in understanding how genes interact with one another. It is the synergistic interplay of genes that generates the genetic programs that control embryogenesis. To understand how such programs evolved, however, is a matter of current research.[8] An improved understanding of how mutations in regulatory genes bring forth new embryonic programs will bring the phenomenon of emergence into focus. It will then become obvious that emergence is the primary cause of organismic evolution, not natural selection. In this way, organic evolution would follow the same logic of the synthetic process already at work in preorganic evolution. The formula for evolution is not *mutation* and selection but *invention* and selection.[9]

Evolution of Consciousness and the "I."   The original big bang explosion of the universe first created the various elements of matter. These particles of "frozen" energy interacted with one another and formed the first "simple" atoms of hydrogen and helium. Out of these, all of the different atoms listed in the periodic chart were synthesized in the various nuclear furnaces of stars. As stars exploded, the synthesized atoms were spewed out into space where they formed gigantic clouds of dust. In these clouds, the atoms could interact with one another to form surprisingly complex molecules. Under the influence of gravity, these dust clouds collapsed to form new stars. Our sun is a star born in this way. Dust from the original cloud, still circling the forming sun, aggregated to form planetesimals. As these collided with one another, the planets formed. On Earth, the presence of abundant water allowed the molecules inherited from space to interact with one another in increasingly complex ways. The energy required for the chemical evolution was provided, at least in part, by the heat generated in the inner parts of the Earth and partially by the sun.

The evolving organic matter passed through the integration of more and more complex molecules to the synthesis of life.

Analogous to the increase in chemical complexity, the various forms of life also became more and more complex. Evolution greatly increased the complexity of life along often precarious, odd, and convoluted paths. Increasing complexity, that is, more efficient integration of diverse organismic structures, led to increased skills to solve problems. One result of complexification in organismic evolution was the emergence of nervous systems. These systems allowed better and better extraction of the energy available in the environment. Thanks to evolving patterns of behavior, organisms could first find favorable niches in the environment and later build such niches. The nests of birds or beaver dens are examples of this process. The capability of organisms to act on their surroundings demonstrates that they can distinguish between themselves and the environment in which they live. Purposeful behavior, organized action to reach a goal, is the sign of consciousness and indicates the level of organismic complexity.

We do not know how consciousness made the "quantum jump" into self-consciousness in human beings. The logic of the evolutionary process would suggest, however, that fundamental psychic elements came to us from our apelike ancestors. It took only about four million years for these creatures (most likely *Australopithecus afarensis*) to evolve into modern human beings (Johanson et al. 1987, 205). Fascinating, touching, and frightening accounts relating to this likely scenario can be found in Jane Goodall's book on chimpanzees (Goodall 1986, 136). They seem so very close to us not only in their affections but also in the wars they fight! The point is that the elements that are integrated into our psyche were synthesized at prehuman levels. From this perspective, the architecture of the human psyche depends on the proper integration of psychic elements at multiple levels. The archetypes discovered and described by C. G. Jung might serve as an example of the importance of unification of psychic entities. Self-consciousness and the appearance of the "I" was the last and highest level reached by the synthetic process of natural evolution. "Thinking existed long before man was able to say: 'I am conscious of thinking'" (Jung [1939] 1968, 280). "The personality of the 'I' depends on the integration of the entire psychic structure" (Jung [1939] 1968, 289).

Philosophy of Evolution.   The advancement of scientific knowledge and its impact on our understanding of the universe demonstrates that the methods of science are practical modes of philosophy. It is a great accomplishment by science to demonstrate, for example, that the universe did not originate from matter nor from spirit but from energy. Science further shows that energy not only "froze" into matter, but that it is also the fundamental agent of cosmic development: without energy, there is no morphogenesis.

In this view, there is only one universal, creative process at work in physical as well as organismic evolution. This process is creative through the integration of diversity into new units. These emerging units might at first be identical but then diversify. Diversification is a result of the fundamental temporospatial nature of the universe. Newly synthesized identical entities will have to occupy niches that cannot be identical anywhere, anytime. Because the emerging new units become part of the different niches they occupy, their modes ("colors") become different from one another. On the level of the evolving matter, this creates differences in the same type of units, polarities necessary for the synthesis of novelty at the next level of complexity.

Complexity that emerges from synthesis unifies diversity. Although the diversity of the integrated elements still exists, the emerging new unity is one. This integrated oneness is unified diversity, simple complexity. Inasmuch as units of integrated complexity are also simple, they can serve as elements for a still more complex unity that might emerge from them in a next synthetic step. The process continues by the synthesis of more and more complex unities from which still more complex entities emerged by synthesis. In my opinion, it is justified to call these increasingly complex levels "higher" levels. The terms *lower* and *higher* express the intensity of synthesis. The more different, contrasting elements a unity integrates, the higher that unity is (Ehrenfels [1890] 1960, 44).

The nature of the universal process of evolution results in a discontinuous and hierarchical organization of reality. The process is discontinuous because each synthetic step creates a new level of reality in a "quantum" jump. The morphogenetic process also creates hierarchy because a synthetic unity orchestrates the activities of its elements. The synthetic unity that emerges in the "I" is perhaps the most powerful example to illustrate this hierarchical "top-down" regulation.

The view that novelty emerges from synthetic events also reveals the basic importance of history because the new cannot be pulled out from the past. History cannot be an extrapolation from the past because the present emerges as genuine novelty from synthetic events. This also explains why knowing all of the parameters of the present will not allow one to predict the future, as Laplace claimed. It is the great accomplishment of Henri Bergson ([1907] 1944) to have seen this deterministic fallacy. In his book, *Creative Evolution*, he showed that the time of the future is not an extrapolation from the time of the past. The future is open—what happens is historical in nature, not an unfolding or a realization of the parameters of the past. In other words, cosmogenesis is essentially a historical process. Therefore, evolution cannot be goal oriented; it cannot be the realization of a blueprint somehow present at the beginning of creation. What actually happens during this history of the cosmos at any one instant is the realization of one event out of an entire horizon of other possible events. The realization of actual events is probabilistic and historic, not deterministic or teleological in nature. Put bluntly, from the perspective of the natural sciences, evolution does not execute a plan to bring forth human beings. I enthusiastically agree with the biologist Stephen J. Gould when he writes, "*Homo sapiens*, I fear, is a thing so small in a vast universe, a wildly improbable evolutionary event well within the realm of contingency. Make of such a conclusion what you will. Some find the prospect depressing; I have always regarded it as exhilarating, and a source of both freedom and consequent moral responsibility" (1989, 291).

II. EVOLUTION AND THE CHRISTIAN DOCTRINE OF CREATION

The fundamental revelation of Christianity is that God is love. God created the world out of love, became human, suffered, died, and rose again so that we might share eternal life (and creation with us). Implicit in this message is that it is universal as well as absolute. Christian theology holds that salvation in Jesus Christ is not relative, limited to one or another epoch only, but rather relevant for all times. This view implies that it can be made believable again and again to all human beings, in spite of changing worldviews. Human beings are different from all other creatures in that they are capable of rational thought. Therefore, one test that religious affirmations must pass is that they have to be reasonable to believe throughout history, including our time. The task is to translate these affirmations into the various human cultures and epochs so that the central point, namely that God is love, remains believable.

This was the task that Hegel faced. During his lifetime, the evidence was fast accumulating that plants and animals had drastically changed overtime and therefore could not have been created in one single act. Hegel closely followed the significant developments in the systematic of animals, for example, the way in which Jean-Baptist Lamarck in France ranked animals (see Hegel [1841] 1964, 9:693-96). It became obvious to Lamarck that higher organisms had somehow developed from less perfect, lower ones. "Under increasing perfection Lamarck understood the gradual increase in 'animality' from the simplest animals to those with the most complex organization, culminating in man" (Mayr 1982, 345).

For Hegel, this must have been an exciting confirmation of the suggestion made by Leibniz that nature was driving toward increased perfection.[10] Hegel defined nature as the Absolute Idea (God) in total difference or "otherness." Hegel writes, "God has two revelations, as nature and as spirit, and both manifestations are temples which He fills, and in which He is present. God as an abstraction is not the true God; His truth is the positing of his other, the living process, the world, which is His Son when comprehended in its divine form" (Hegel [1827] 1970, 204). God is not limited by "otherness." "Otherness" within God is the Son, united with the Father in the Holy Spirit. "Otherness" outside of God is nature, creation. Nature is the Son of God, not as Son however but as abiding "otherness" (Hegel [1827] 1970, 206). Within God, the Spirit is by itself through the Father and the Son. Outside of God, the Spirit is outside of itself. In this mode of "otherness," the Spirit is the furthest away from being itself because it is not by itself. This sets the creative process in motion through which the Spirit transmutates from level to level until it comes to itself, comes to possess itself in the freedom of humankind. The fulfillment of this freedom is to be able to respond to God's love freely, not forced in any way. Ultimately, the true love of God for humanity and the genuine loving response of humankind to God becomes real in Jesus Christ. He is, as the Son of Man, the Son of God (Hegel [1809/1811] 1961, 3:226; [1845] 1965, 19:132-34). As the New Adam, Christ shows the face of God in human form. The image of God becomes (again) visible in him. This image is not just a picture of God but the appearance of God (*imago Dei*) in the "otherness" of humans. On the face of this image, the "otherness" of God appears as all that is created, all that is not God, thanks to God. This is how Hegel sees the relationship between God and the creation. It is the relationship of love in which "otherness" provides the polarity that is encouraged, enjoyed, and celebrated.

The passage just cited from Hegel—"His truth is the positing of his other, the living process, the world"—might be a misleading choice of terms. Hegel does not understand "process" mechanistically, in the sense of a process that executes the Creator's plan. This is why he refers to this process from which the world originates as "the living process." According to Hegel, nature, that is, creation, is the "otherness" of God outside of God. Within God, "otherness" is the Son (of God). Outside of God, "otherness" is nature, the Son of God outside of God, namely, Jesus Christ, God and man in the unity of one person. This unity is neither reduction of Christ's humanity into God nor the disintegration of the Son of God into the Son of Man. Rather, it is the ultimate unity in the difference, the Son of God and the Son of Man, the affirmation of the total diversity of both, yet in genuine unity. The point is that nature is not God but the "otherness" of God. God that is God but outside of God. In this way, nature can be itself.

This understanding of the nature of nature is anchored in various passages of the New Testament, for example in Saint Paul's letter to the Corinthians (1 Cor. 8:6), to the Colossians (Col. 1:16-17), Hebrews (Heb. 1:2), and especially in the prologue to the Gospel of Saint John (John 1:1-3). "In the beginning was the Word and the Word was with God, and the Word was God" (the expression of God within God, the Son). "He was in the beginning with God. All things (creation) came to be through him, and without him, nothing came to be. What came to be through him was life."

This brings us back to Hegel's understanding of creation as "living process" that creates the world. It is the unity of the spirit that assures that nature can be one, can become what it is, namely, a unity that through the living process will ultimately become itself, possess itself, so that it can be free. It is "otherness" of God outside of God that through the living (not mechanical) process becomes itself. The ultimate difference between God and nature expressed as "otherness" cannot provide any ground for God to become, to develop together with the world. For Hegel, nature is not part of God, or God part of nature. Nature is the "otherness" of God outside of God.

Outside of God, there is not anything, no eternal matter, no chaos, only nothing. There is nothing because pure being is pure abstraction, the absolute negative, which is nothing. What is has already passed over into nothing and nothing into being. This vanishing into its opposite is the essence of becoming. Becoming is the movement in which both (pure being and pure nothing) vanish into their opposite. Their truth is the movement of the immediate vanishing of the one in the other. Becoming is the movement in which pure being and pure nothing are distinguished but by a difference, which has equally immediately resolved itself (Hegel [1812] 1969, 82-83).

Hegel's reflection on the nature of pure being (namely, that it is nothing) integrates another essential Christian understanding of creation—that God created the world out of nothing.[11] "In the beginning God created Heaven and Earth." This first point in the Apostles' Creed makes it impossible to ponder the problem of creation outside this fundamental revelation, namely, that God is independent from His creation but not vice versa (Barth [1958] 1977, 3). The point is that the Christian God is not in a process of becoming. The world is not a pantheistic God, nor is creation part of a panentheistic Creator.

Hegel's notion of nature as the "otherness" of God outside of God does not deify nature, nor does the divine become part of the process of creation. Both misunderstandings originate because "otherness" is reduced to "sameness in difference" and not left as (radical) "otherness" as the abyss between God and His creation that only the Almighty God can bridge in Jesus Christ.

For Christians, there can be no doubt that God created the universe: Holy Scripture begins with this bold statement. It is not an accident that this is the first sentence in the Bible: all that follows is based on the acceptance of this basic relationship between God and His creation. The sentence can leave no doubt in the reader's mind that God existed "before" and independently from His creation. God is God without creation. God is not less God because creation was not, nor does God need creation to become God. The revelation of God's plan of salvation that unfolds from this first sentence in the Bible on to the death and resurrection of Jesus Christ is anchored in the freedom of God to act. This freedom is absolute, not restricted by whether creation is or is not. The perspective from process theology that God depends on the creation, in any way becomes together with the world, is not the Hegelian view. Hegel's philosophy of nature is firmly rooted in the fundamental Christian revelation that God is independent of the world, is the free, the omnipotent, the supreme being that creates creation not out of any necessity or constraints but out of love.

The love of God appears in history in the person of Jesus Christ, the Savior of the world. Christians know that God has a plan for His creation, namely, to save it through the death and resurrection of Jesus Christ. Christ is the fulfillment and purpose not only of human history but of the history of all creation.

Based on the fundamental Christian dogma that God is love, Hegel incorporated the science of his time into a philosophy of nature. In so doing, the history of nature, including the history of human beings, was understood as the realization of God's plan. In this way, the outcome of history was already given at the start. History became a historic because what happened was not really creative but mere actualizations of what had already been fixed. In Hegel's system, one might argue, there is no real history, only teleological reaching of the goal that was already given in the past.

This, however, is not the history of the ever-involved, ever-present, ever-creating, graceful, and loving Christian God. Here we face the Christian paradox that God is involved in all cosmic and human history but in ways that do not prevent creation from becoming itself. On the one hand, God is intimately involved in His creation, is at the center of its becoming, yet lets creation, and with it human beings, become themselves in freedom. A shadow of God's nature falls on those who raise children: what a constant involvement in letting go!

This might well be the center of the problem for a current Christian doctrine of creation: how can creation create itself and still fulfill God's plan? In trying to answer this fundamental question, we are in danger of equating our human ways of planning with the way God acts. God does not impose plans on creation by intervening at "critical stages" of the process. God does not act in history by creating something first and then later introducing modifications. God creates not only "out of nothing" (ex nihilo) but also "without movement" (sine motu, Thomas Aquinas, Summa Theologiae, I, 45, 3). Therefore, God does not guide the natural creative process by imposing God's ways. Rather, by letting the natural process create itself freely, it precisely fulfills God's plan. Again, we are at the center of Christian revelation that is clearly paradoxical for the human mind. Langdon Gilkey touches the heart of this matter when he writes, "He gives being, but not His own being; that He is eternal, and yet He founds and rules time; that He is infinite, absolute, unconditioned, and self-sufficient, and yet that He limits Himself by a dependent creature outside of Him; that He is in all as their ground, and yet over against all as their personal judge and savior; that He is good, and yet permits the existence of real evil. Each paradox cries for a resolution; it seems to leave us with an intellectual conflict unsupportable by a rational mind" (1959, 280).

We can obtain a glimpse into the way God Almighty plans by pondering the actions of the persons involved in the history of Christ's passion. They are not marionettes in the hand of God—that would have been a thin and superficial plot indeed! Judas, Pilate, as well as the High Priest freely follow their own plans and are not captives of a scheme imposed by God. God the Almighty executes plans in ways that we cannot: God's plans are fulfilled through human beings acting freely. As they execute their plots, God's plan is fulfilled with ultimate precision.

God's plan of salvation is fulfilled through human beings acting freely. In analogous ways, so does creation fulfill God's will by creating itself freely by its own laws. Just as for the unbeliever, there is no saving plan that is realized in Christ's passion; so outside of faith, evolution does not fulfill any purpose. Thus, for science, there is no plan, no teleology, and no goal toward which evolution works its way. The insight that there is a God who has a plan for the creation is given by faith, not natural history. Although there is this strong desire to see faith confirmed by science, Christians know that faith does not have its roots in science. Time and time again, they have had to learn the lesson that nature is capable of creating itself. Time and time again, faith had to withdraw from the entanglement with science because science had made progress and came to understand what previously had to be "explained by faith."[12] Christians will have to let go of this new unfaithfulness to faith, this attempt to justify faith by science. That creation has a purpose is a matter of true faith, not science. Faith comes to itself only in its own realm. It is the reality created through the experience of Christian life. Faith cannot become an integral part of a philosophical system because the freedom of the loving God and the freedom of the lovingly responding human beings cannot be locked into a system. Hegel's philosophy of nature limits the history of nature because it understands cosmogenesis as a process that is goal oriented from the start. Proceeding toward a predetermined end, however, restricts the importance of historical events. History as the sequence of probabilistic, reality-creating events degenerates into a sequential execution of an already given schedule. I doubt whether Hegel understood the development of nature in this teleological way, but his philosophy of nature was frequently understood in this manner. Science has shown since Hegel that there is natural history but no natural teleology. This lesson learned from the book of nature illustrates that human beings are not the predetermined outcome of a plan but a historic, probabilistic, creative event of nature. Philip Hefner (1992, 337) is at the heart of the matter when he writes, "Homo sapiens is to be understood as part of nature's process, not only ecologically, but in terms of kinship with all that has appeared within the process of nature's evolution." Thanks to the freedom of nature to create itself, human beings are free. The freedom of human beings and the freedom of nature to create itself cannot be limited in any way. Evolution is essential for the Christian doctrine of creation because it safeguards the freedom of human beings and the creation for which they stand (Mark 8:18-24).

The Russian theologian and philosopher Vladimir Solovyev (1851-1900) may have been the first to see this. He finds the point of departure for thinking over the relationship between God and the creation in contemplating the theological understanding of the relationship between Christ and the church. The church is born on Good Friday as Christ gives Himself up for her by His death. In this mystical way, the church becomes Christ's body in which all the believers are members. The church and Christ are one, but it is oneness in difference. It is the oneness of bridegroom and bride, true unity that is one in the difference. It is the oneness experienced by persons embracing one another, spouses united in the same spirit. This is the relationship between Christ and the church, it is one that is inclusive of difference, for Christ is not the church and the church is not Christ, but they are one precisely in this difference.

How this can be is the mystery of love. In human love, we experience this structure of identity in the difference. In love between persons, the persons are always different yet become one. Such is the loving relationship between Christ and His church. It should also be the structure of the universal church. The church, the bride of Christ, can only be one but again, a oneness in united diversity. It is in this way that all human beings, with all their differences, can be this church. It is thanks to this diversity of human beings united in the spirit of Christ that the church is one. True unity is inclusive, not exclusive of diversity. And although there are limits to the integrative power of human love, there are no limits in unifying diversity for the love of God. It is with a confession of this omnipotent power of God's love that the Christian Creed begins, "We believe in one God, the Father, the Almighty" (Solovyev, [1889] 1948, 147).

Solovyev then reflects on what this means, namely, to say that God is almighty. He writes,

> God exists in Himself and by Himself. The reality He possesses is in the first place altogether from within; it is an absolute substance. So too the proper action or essential manifestation of God cannot be either determined or modified by any external cause, but is simply the pure and perfect (that is, completely adequate) reproduction of His own being, His unique substance. This reproduction cannot be either a new creation or a division of the divine substance; it cannot be created because it exists from all eternity, it cannot be divided because it is not a material thing, but pure actuality. God, possessing Himself, manifests it for Himself, and reproduces Himself in a purely interior act. By this act He arrives at the enjoyment of Himself, that is, of His absolute substance, not only as existing, but also as manifested. Thus the complete existence of God does not require Him to go outside Himself, nor does it set Him in any external relationship; it is perfect in itself, and does not involve the existence of anything outside itself. In the three constituent modes of His being, God is in unique relation to His own substance: 1) He possesses it in Himself, in His "first act" (absolute fact). 2) He possesses it in Himself, in manifesting or producing it from Himself in His "second act" (absolute action). 3) He possesses it in returning upon Himself, in rediscovering in it a "third act", the perfect unity of His being and His manifestation (absolute

enjoyment). He cannot enjoy it without having manifested it, and He cannot manifest it without having it in Himself. Thus three acts, states or relationships—here the terms coincide—indissolubly bound together, are different but equal expressions of the entire Godhead. ([1889] 1948, 148)

Solovyev continues by identifying and naming these three coeternal equal expressions (hypostases) of the entire Godhead Father, Son, and Holy Spirit. The unity of the Father, the unity in being, is actively manifested in the Son, the direct action (the word) of the Father both united in this difference by the Holy Spirit ([1889] 1948, 157).

Solovyev follows here Hegel's reflections on the triune God. God is omnipotent, that is, not limited, because God is the absolute difference within Himself. This is Hegel's "otherness" of God within God. For Solovyev, outside of God is chaos, that is, total absence of form. There we have reached the point of origin of creation, namely, chaos as the pure possibility of being. Without being anything in particular, chaos "is" nothing at all. God the Almighty, however, wants to give room to chaos, wants chaos, the antithesis of God, to become reality. God wants to give existence to what is outside of God, embrace what is not God. Chaos has a chance to become something because God's love is so powerful that He gives existence away. With this gift of existence, creation can become itself. Thanks to this gift of existence, the gift of creation genuinely given, really turned over to creation. In this way, creation is free to become itself. Here is perhaps the critical difference between Hegel and Solovyev. For Hegel, the path of nature is predetermined. It is the spirit that step-by-step ascends toward becoming itself. Within nature, there is this Lamarckian drive toward increased perfection. Solovyev avoided this pitfall. He studied and deeply admired Charles Darwin's work, which had made such a powerful case that nature could create itself. Within nature, there is this Lamarckian drive toward increased perfection.

Solovyev avoided this pitfall. He studied and deeply admired Charles Darwin's work,[15] which made such a powerful case that nature could create itself. "Why are the labors and efforts necessary in the life of the world," Solovyev writes,

> Why must nature experience the pains of birth, and why, before it can generate the perfect and eternal organism, must it produce so many ugly, monstrous broods, which are unable to endure the struggle for existence and perish without a trace? Why does God

leave nature to reach her goals so slowly and by such ill means? Why in general, is the realization of divine idea in the world a gradual and complex process, and not a single, simple act? The full answer to this question is contained in one word, which expresses something without which neither God nor nature can be conceived; the word is *freedom*. ([1873] 1948, 179)[16]

This brings us back to the passage from Stephen J. Gould's work cited earlier. Divine freedom and human freedom are indeed the prerequisites for the Christian understanding of the relationship between the Creator and His creation. Love is freely offered and has to be freely returned—there is no other loving way.

By taking Darwin's discovery that evolution works by natural selection of favorable variations seriously, Solovyev moved away from the progressive, Hegel-Lamarckian view of nature. This opened the possibility to see nature as becoming itself, not forced by any drive imposed on it. By forcing neither world nor God, Solovyev remained closely in the realm of love. His point is that creation originates in the love of God, who creates creation in such a way that it can create itself! That this is really so is the basic lesson the scientists of all ages learned from studying the book of nature. It beautifully confirms the basic point of Holy Scripture, namely, that God is love.

Out of love, God gives to creation the gift to create itself. Genuinely given gifts, somehow, reflect the nature of the giver. From the evolution of matter to the evolution of life, including human beings, their art and culture, it is synthesis that creates.[17] The ontological structure of all that is, is identity in the difference, unity in diversity.

That all creation is structured in this way might be a reflection of the Trinitarian nature of the Creator.

NOTES

1. Recently, an exciting result was reported that corroborates the big bang model. The original explosion generated tremendous heat that can still be measured today. Mapping of the temperature differences that still exist in space illustrates that the universe is still hotter in the central, equatorial regions as compared with polar areas. The map also shows unequal distribution of heat, most likely due to the turbulence in matter that "froze" from energy. For a picture of this map, see *Nature* 356, 741 (1992).

2. For an entry into more recent literature on nucleosynthesis, see *Nature* 357, 379-84 (1992).

3. This is not advocating teleology because there is no program that could guide cosmic evolution. There are goal-oriented processes in nature, such as embryonic development or purposeful behavior of organisms. Both, however, are dependent on genetic programs. Ernst Mayr classifies such program-guided processes as *teleonomic* processes (Mayr 1982, 48.) For processes that are not guided by a program yet have a predictable outcome because of physical law, Mayr uses the term *teleomatic* processes. He gives the example of a falling rock on a mountain slope that bounces toward the valley. Mayr writes, "The entire process of cosmic evolution, from the first big bang to the present time, is strictly due to a sequence of teleomatic processes on which stochastic processes are superimposed" (1982, 49). I disagree with Mayr on this point because the falling rock example is an example for the behavior of closed systems. In such systems, order decreases while entropy increases. They move toward equilibrium, the lowest possible energetic state. Cosmic evolution, however, happens in a system that drives ultimately on the energy released in the original explosion of the big bang. Evolution is the result of an energy input, not energy output, as in the example of the falling rock. I agree with Mayr that cosmogenesis is a probabilistic, historic process. This process, however, is not teleomatic but morphogenetic. For morphogenetic yet probabilistic processes, I suggest the term *teleomorphic* processes (Brun 1994).

4. For current information, see *Science* 256, 1396 (1992).

5. Ernst Mayr (1982, 63) gives a short history of emergentism in biology. He also points out that two false claims against this view have to be rejected: it is not a vitalistic concept and does not deny the necessity to study nature by trying to understand its parts. Emergentism points out that complex systems must be studied at all levels of their organization. This is so because complex unities are integrated entities—they are, therefore, hierarchically organized.

   It is important to point out, however, that this view is stressing the importance of the Gestalt concept, namely, that the whole has qualities that are not present in its parts. The concept is probably rooted in organismic wholes already studied by Aristotle and later expanded to all unity, for example, in the monadology of Leibniz. Borrowing from Leibniz and Spinoza, the concept of wholeness (or Gestalt) became the key concept in the works of Goethe as well as Hegel.

6. Variation and selection are the two components of organismic evolution. In my opinion, there is an analogous phenomenon to "selection" in physical evolution: physical entities (atoms, molecules, etc.) can only exist ("survive") in stable states within mathematical landscapes.

7.   Michael E. Akam (*Nature* 362 [1993]:509) points to this reductionist language when he writes, "It is a profound error to equate a mutation that changes the symmetry of torsion (in a snail) with a mutation that invents the mechanism of torsion itself. This is like saying that all the genetic difference between male and female, oogenesis and spermatogenesis, are specified by a single gene on the Y chromosome. This may be true at the population level, but it tells us absolutely nothing about the developmental complexity of the process itself."

8.   See Kauffman (1993) and references therein, particularly the chapter entitled "Order and Ontogeny," pp. 407-520.

9.   For an elaboration of this view and its implication for the arts, see Brun (1993, 1994).

10.   Leibniz writes, "Although many substances have already attained a great perfection, yet on account of the infinite divisibility of the continuous, there always remain in the abyss of things slumbering parts which have yet to be awakened, to grow in size and worth, and in a word, to advance to a more perfect state . . . there is a perpetual and most free progress of the whole universe in fulfillment of the universal beauty and perfection of the works of God, so that it is always advancing towards a greater development" (cited from Ernst Mayr 1982, 324).

11.   Part of the Jewish inheritance that determined Christian understanding of creation came from the Genesis texts in the Old Testament. There, God the Creator creates by the power of His word alone. This is in striking contrast to the understanding of other (Greek) cosmologies. There, the Creator created the world out of matter which was thought to be coeternal with God. For a history of the doctrine of creation out of nothing, see Gerhard May (1978).

12.   Perhaps the most painful retreat of faith so far was the replacement of William Paley's divine designer by Darwin's discovery of natural selection. God, the Creator of all of the wondrously adapted living beings, was replaced by evolution that simply followed natural law: faith was replaced by science. Each time there was significant scientific progress in our understanding of how the world works, God's action in this world became less necessary. But there were still gaps in our understanding of how the world works. Gaps, such as how humankind originated or how life began on earth, that could only be explained by God's action. Painfully, we have come to understand that such gaps are not the proof of God's intervention but that they only seem to exist because we are still lacking in our understanding of how nature works. The "God of the gaps" was the God introduced "to explain areas of scientific ignorance, and destined to retreat in the light of new knowledge to become the Retired Architect, the inactive God of Deism" (Barbour 1966, 43).

13. For biographical information on Vladimir Solovyev, see the introduction to Solovyev's *Lectures on Godmanhood* by Peter Zouboff.

14. For Solovyev, the unification of the Eastern and Western churches into the one church, the spouse of Christ, was an urgent task to be accomplished. He worked very hard for the unification of the Orthodox Church of Russia with the Church of Rome. He made it clear that he did not understand unification as a merger. The Church of the East and the one of the West did not have to disappear into one another but should be harmonized into the true unity of the one universal church (Frank 1950, 75).

15. Solovyev admired Darwin, especially for his views, as expressed in *The Descent of Man*, about the origin of beauty in nature. See Frank (1950) 136.

16. Solovyev clearly saw the importance of safeguarding the freedom of creation in order to safeguard the freedom of humanity to enter into a loving relationship with its Creator. He made his point in his lectures at the University of Moscow in 1876 by using the detailed information he had obtained from Darwin's major works: *Origin of Species*, published in 1859, and *The Descent of Man,* which became available in 1871.

17. The Neoplatonic emphasis on the One, the insight that unification creates novelty, has been integrated into Christian thought by the fathers of the church. For example, Saint Augustine writes ([ca. 391] 1991, 169), "To be truly formed is to be brought into a unity. For what is supremely one is the principle of all form."

    The insight that synthesis creates is central for the work of Father Teilhard de Chardin. On November 4, 1917, he wrote, "For union is the creative process" and "to create is to unite" (cited from de Lubac 1971, 15).

REFERENCES

Augustine. *[ca. 393] 1991. On the Literal Interpretation of Genesis: An Unfinished Book.* In *The Fathers of the Church: A New Translation.* Washington D.C.: The Catholic University of America Press.

Aquinas, Thomas. *Summa theologiae.* Latin text and English translation. Vol. Ia, 34-39, ed. Thomas Gilbey, O. P. Blackfriars. New York: McGraw-Hill.

Bachmann, P. A., P. L. Luisi, and J. Lang. 1992. "Autocatlytic Self-replicating Micelles as Models for Prebiotic Structures." *Nature* 357: 57-59.

Barbour, I. G. 1966. *Issues in Science and Religion.* New York: Harper and Row.

Barth, K. [1958] 1977. *Church Dogmatics.* Vol. 3: *The Doctrine of Creation,* part 1. Authorized translation by G. T. Thomson and others. Edinburgh: Klark.

Bergson, H. [1907] 1944. *L'Evolution Créatrice.* Paris: Flamarion. Translated by Arthur Mitchell as *Creative Evolution.* New York: Random House.

Brooks, D. R., and E. O. Wiley. 1986. *Evolution as Entropy*. Chicago: Univ. of Chicago Press.

Brun, R. B. 1993. "Principles of Morphogenesis in Embryonic Development, Music and Evolution." *Communio* 20 (Fall 1993): 528-43.

————. 1994. "Nature, Life and Art" (under review).

Cairns-Smith, A. G. 1982. *Genetic Takeover and the Mineral Origins of Life*. New York: Cambridge Univ. Press. de Lubac, H. [1968] 1971. *The Eternal Feminine: A Study on the Poem by Teilhard de Chardin*. London: Collins.

Ehrenfels, C. von. [1890] 1960. *Höhe und Reinheit der Gestalt*. In *Gestalthaftes Sehen, Ergebnisse und Aufgaben der Morphologie*. Zum Hundertjährigen Geburtstag von Christian von Ehrenfels. ed. Ferdinand Weinhandl. Darmstadt: Wissenschaftl. Buchgesellschaft.

Engel, M. H., S. A. Macko, and J. A. Silfer. 1990. "Carbon Isotope Composition of Individual Amino Acids in the Murchinson meteorite." *Nature* 348 (November): 47-49.

Fowler, W. A. 1984. *The Quest for the Origin of the Elements*. Science 226 (November): 922-35.

Frank, S. L. 1950. *A Solovyev Anthology*. New York: Scribner's Sons.

Gilkey, L. 1959. *Maker of Heaven and Earth: A Study of the Christian Doctrine of Creation*. New York: Doubleday.

Goldschmidt, R. [1940] 1960. *The Material Basis of Evolution*. Paterson, N.J.: Pageant Books.

Goodall, J. 1986. *The Chimpanzees of Gambe: Patterns of Behavior*. Cambridge: Cambridge Univ. Press.

Gould, S. J. 1980. "Is a New Theory of Evolution Emerging" *Palaeobiology* 6 (Winter): 119-30.

————. 1989. Wonderful Life. New York: W. W. Norton.

Graham, L. R. 1972. *Science and Philosophy in the Soviet Union*. New York: Knopf.

Hanawalt, P. C. 1980. *Molecules to Living Cells: Readings from Scientific American*. San Francisco: Freeman.

Hefner, Philip. 1992. "Nature, God's Great Project." *Zygon: Journal of Religion and Science* 27 (September): 327-41.

Hegel, G. W. F. [1812] 1969. *Hegel's Science of Logic*. Translated by A. V. Miller. Second edition. New York: Humanities Press.

————. [1827] 1970. Philosophy of Nature. Edited and translated by M. J. Petry. London: Humanities Press.

_____. [1809/1811, published in 1840] 1961. Philosophische Propädeutik. Sämtliche Werke, Band 3. Vierte Auflage der Jubiläumsausgabe, Stuttgart: Friedrich Frommann Verlag.

_____. [1841] 1964. System der Philosophie. Zweiter Teil: Die Naturphilosophie. Sämtliche Werke, Band 9. Vierte Auflage der Jubiläumsausgabe. Stuttgart-Bad Cannstatt: Friedrich Frommann Verlag.

_____. [1845] 1965. Vorlesungeng über die Geschichte der Philosophie, Dritter Band. Sämtliche Werke, Band 19. Vierte Auflage der Jubiläumsausgabe. Stuttgart-Bad Cannstatt: Friedrich Frommann Verlag.

Ingham, P. W. 1988. "The Molecular Genetics of Embryonic Pattern Formation in Drosophila." *Nature* 335 (September): 25-34.

Johanson, D. C., T. M. Fidelis, G. G. Eck, T. D. White, R. C. Walter, W. H. Kimbel, B. Asfaw, P. Manega, P. Ndessokia, and G. Suwa. 1987. "New Partial Skeleton of *Homo habilis* from Olduvai Gorge, Tanzania." *Nature* 327 (May): 205-9.

Jung, C. G. [1939] 1968. *The Archetypes and the Collective Unconsciousness.* Vol. 9, part 1, of *The Collected works of C. G. Jung.* Bollingen series XX: Second edition. Princeton, NJ: Princeton Univ. Press.

Kauffman, S. A. 1993. *The Origins of Order, Self-Organization and Selection in Evolution.* New York: Oxford Univ. Press.

Margulis, L. 1984. *Early Life.* Boston: Jones & Bartlett.

May, G. 1978 *Schöpfung aus dem Nichts.* In *Arbeiten zur Kirchengeschichte.* Berlin: Walter de Gruyter.

Mayr, E. 1982. *The Growth of Biological Thought.* Cambridge: Harvard Univ. Press.

Ohno, S. 1970. *Evolution by Gene Duplication.* New York: Springer Verlag.

Prigogine, I. 1980. *From Being to Becoming: Time and Complexity in the Physical Sciences.* San Francisco: Freeman.

Raff, R. A., and E. C. Raff. 1985. *Development as an Evolutionary Process.* Proceedings of a meeting held at the Marine Biological Laboratory in Woods Hole, Massachusetts, August 23 and 24. Lectures in Biology, vol. 8, 203-28. New York: MBL.

Solovyev, V. [1873] 1948. *Lectures on Godmanhood.* London: Dennis Dobson.

_____. [1889] 1948. Russia and the Universal Church. London: G. Bles.

Weinberg, S. 1977. *The First Three Minutes: A Modern View of the Origin of the Universe.* New York: Basic Books.

TRANSCENDENTALISM OR EMPIRICISM? A DISCUSSION ON A PROBLEM RAISED IN E. O. WILSON'S BOOK CONSILIENCE

(*Zygon*, vol. 40, no. 3 [September 2005])

Abstract.   E. O. Wilson writes that the "choice between transcendentalism and empiricism" is this century's "version of the struggle for men's soul" (1998, 240). The transcendentalist argues for theism—that there is a God, a Creator of the world. The empiricist instead makes the point that the notion of God, including morality and ethics, are adaptive structures of human evolution. Before entering the debate of the transcendentalist/empiricist controversy, I analyze how things exist and suggest that all that is exists as united diversity, as identity in difference. I argue that oneness by itself is intangible because wholes are concrete only through their tangible parts. I briefly discuss this understanding of existence in the realm of art to show that transcendence and immanence are not mutually exclusive but constitute each other. I conclude that existence, the hypostasis of unity in diversity, might be seen as a gift from absolute existence. In this view, the world might reveal itself as a gift that reflects the Trinitarian existence of the Giver.

In this essay, I enter into the discussion between empiricists and transcendentalists. E. O. Wilson writes, "The choice between transcendentalism and empiricism will be the coming's century's version of the struggle for men's soul" (1998, 240). I think he is right: the trouble in bridging the gap between science and religion is the difficulty of harmonizing the empiricist's positions with the transcendentalist's views. It is a central problem that already came into the foreground when comparing the materialist understanding of the world with essentialist views—Democritus with Plato, for example.

Descartes attempted to bridge the abyss between these two contrasting positions. He suggested that God created matter and set it in motion "and then lent his concurrence to enable nature to operate as it normally does" (Descartes [1637] 1988, 42). Descartes had to publish his work anonymously because the Roman Inquisition had just condemned Galileo. In Descartes' work published posthumously, he argued that the many changes that one observes in nature could not be properly attributed to the actions of God. This was because, according to the church's doctrine, God's action never changes. Therefore, changes had to occur according to the laws of nature (Descartes [1664] 1985, 93).

I understand Descartes to put forth a deistic understanding of creation: God creates matter in motion and natural law, and these guide creation toward the predetermined goal set by the Creator.

Charles Darwin ([1859] 1902) showed that such a deistic, rather mechanical model was incapable of explaining evolution. In one long argument, he made the case that organisms could not have evolved according to a preconceived plan. Rather, plants and animals came into being through genuine natural history, peppered with accidents and extinctions, not supernatural guidance. Nature evolved by natural means, not by supernatural concurrence. Therefore, the natural process of accidental variation and natural selection could not reach a predetermined goal.

To this day, the transcendentalist opponents of such an empiricist view believe instead that God created the world with a goal in mind and for a purpose. If they accept evolution by natural law at all, they believe that God either constantly guides the process or intervenes in it at least occasionally during critical stages (for variations of this model, see Russell 1993, 1-32). One such critical stage would have been during the original explosion, the big bang. In this case, God would have fine-tuned natural law and constants in such a way that life and human beings could evolve (Barrow and Tipler 1986).

The stakes are high in deciding these matters for one's personal life. If God exists and created the world, we humans are a part of God's creation. If God brought forth the laws that organize the universe, God might also be the author of the moral laws supposed to guide and organize our lives. How can one obtain a defendable, reasonable position on these crucial issues?

I want to follow E. O. Wilson's example and also lay my cards face up on the table. I agree with Wilson's transcendentalist who wonders, like many philosophers and theologians before, "Why is there something instead of nothing?" (Wilson 1998, 242). This fundamental question originates from the experience that human beings are obviously not the creators of the universe. The belief that a supreme being that transcends the world created it, including us, is the foundation of transcendentalism. It attests that the Creator instituted the laws of nature and, with them, also the laws of moral guidance. God created "the starry heavens above me and the moral law in me," as Immanuel Kant piously confessed ([1788] 1977, 133).

Kant showed that human comprehension must work within the limits imposed on it by time and space, that we cannot reach reality as it is in and by itself. We cannot rid ourselves from the constraints of our mind to comprehend reality from God's perspective. We, therefore, have no hope to ever grasp reality objectively because the world we understand is really but a construct of our subjective mind. Kant compared his discovery to the Copernican revolution. The sun does not circle around the Earth, but instead the Earth revolves around the sun; so our knowledge cannot conform to objects, but objects must conform to our knowledge ([1788] 1977, 148-50).

This raised the problem whether the notion of God was also just a fabrication of the human mind. If so, how could God's objective existence be demonstrated? Kant asserted that it was impossible for human beings to attain speculative or theoretical knowledge of God. This insight, however, opened up the space of faith, the certitude that God existed. Not theoretical reason but the desire of practical reason was the faculty given to human beings to acknowledge the existence of God. Such desire provided the certitude that God—the highest, most perfect, eternal, all-powerful, omniscient, omnipresent Creator of the world—existed. For Kant, this was certain because God was the originator of moral law. He called it the "categorical imperative" given to all human beings. It states, "Act only on that maxim through which you can at the same time will that it should become a universal law" ([1788] 1977, 112). Obviously, there is tension between pure and practical reason. On the one hand, the world is a construct of the mind. On the other, God's (objective) existence is certain and acknowledged by practical (moral) reason.

It did not take long to release this Kantian tension. Roughly fifty years later, in the mid-nineteenth century, Ludwig Feuerbach declared that the notion of God was nothing more than a phantom of the human mind, "The divine being is nothing else than the human being, or, rather the human nature purified freed from the limits of the individual man, made objective i.e., contemplated and revered as another, a distinct being" ([1841] 1975, 14). "*Theology is anthropology:* in other words, the object of religion which in Greek we call *theos* and in our language God, express nothing more than the deified essence of man, so that the history of religion or, what amounts to the same thing, of God—for the gods are as varied as the religions, and the religions are as varied as mankind—is nothing other than the history of man" ([1851] 1967, 17). The deified essence of humanity contains all the powers that self-centered humanity wishes to have. Like humans, the gods are egotistic and therefore must be appeased and worshiped. "Since the gods command over life and death, fortune and misfortune, therefore ethics, the theoretical and practical distinction between good and evil, right and wrong, have been linked to them and their cult" ([1851] 1967, 297).

Modern insights into the origin of religion support Feuerbach's view. "An estimated one hundred thousand belief systems have existed in history, and many fostered ethnic and tribal wars . . . . All great civilizations were spread by conquest, and among their chief beneficiaries were the religions validating them . . . . But every major religion today is a winner in the Darwinian struggle waged among cultures and none ever flourished by tolerating its rivals" (Wilson 1998, 244).

The Darwinian struggle is the struggle for resources. Survival of any human group depends upon having the means necessary to produce and support its members and their offspring. Competition for such resources favors those groups in which individuals cooperate. Cooperation provides a critical advantage in the battle for rich territory with other groups. "Conquest by a tribe requires that its members make sacrifices to the interest of the group, especially during conflict with competing groups. That is simply the expression of a primal rule of social life throughout the animal kingdom. It arises when loss of personal advantage by submission to the needs of the group is more than offset by gain in personal advantage due to the resulting success of the group" (Wilson 1998, 245).

In a nutshell, the empiricist's view is that religion and morality are adaptive outcomes of human evolution. They evolved because they increased the chance of human groups and societies to beat competing groups over the head more efficiently. Human history is peppered with religious, racist, and tribal wars. Genocidal slaughters in Cambodia, Rwanda, Bosnia, and Darfur provide a few current examples. Racist struggles are going on right under the surface of any society. In-group understandings that conflict with outside groups become readily inflamed by religion. How many times disciples of different religions slaughtered one another for the "love" of God!

Taking all of these into account, does the empiricist's argument fully make the case? Transcendentalists might answer like the one in Wilson's book does: "Confine your thoughts to the material world if you wish. Others know that

God encompasses the ultimate causes of Creation. Where do the laws of nature come from if not a power higher than the laws themselves? Science offers no answer to that sovereign question of theology" (1998, 242).

I disagree with this particular point of Wilson's transcendentalist because I think science *does* offer an answer to his question.

Transcendentalism or Empiricism? The View from Science

Over the last few decades, cosmologists and particle physicists have made tremendous progress in tracing the origin of natural laws. Within the first fraction of a second gravity split from the strong, the weak, and the electromagnetic force, at this time, those three forces were still unified. Then the strong force (it holds the atomic nuclei together) splits from the electroweak force and the still-unified electromagnetic and weak force. The electroweak force then splits into the electromagnetic force—the union of magnetism and electricity—and the weak force that controls radioactive decay (Chaisson and McMillan 1999, 629). The point is that the laws of nature did not originate from beyond nature but emerged in time, from within the history of the universe. A speculation here is that a sequence might have unfolded differently, leading to "zillions of universes" (Overbye 2003) with natural laws (and constants) different from ours.

I have a wonderful friend and colleague in the chemistry department who, half jokingly, claims that chemistry is the central science. It took me some time to fully appreciate his point, which is that among all the sciences, chemistry demonstrates most convincingly how novelty emerges from syntheses. Integration of atoms and molecules can bring forth new compounds with totally different properties as compared to the elements from which they were synthesized. A simple example is the synthesis of table salt ($NaCl$) that is obviously very different from either sodium (a metal) or chlorine (a gas).

Complexification

Nature generates new things through bringing together entities that it generated before. Even after degeneration and disasters, the elements left over may become integrated into novelty. The formation of galaxies, for example, is driven by cannibalism, collisions, and other tumultuous events (West et al. 2004); planetary systems may form from the dust cloud left over from stars that exploded (Lissauer 2002). Natural history is the history brought forth by sequential syntheses. Therefore, sequential "dissection" of complexity—whether physical, chemical, or organismic—leads to the isolation of ever-older parts. Single-cell organisms are older than multicellular ones, atoms are older than molecules, and nuclear particles are older than atoms.

Sequential syntheses brought forth not only the physical universe but also life. How it evolved on Earth and perhaps elsewhere is a matter of current research. Our understanding of how nature brought forth all the different forms of life is also still fragmentary. Laboratory experiments and fieldwork demonstrate that the Darwinian mechanism of chance and natural selection ("survival of the fittest") played, and still plays, a crucial role. Today, genetics has gained significant insight into the evolution of genomes. We now know that duplications of already existing genes increased the number of available genes. Some of these mutated to produce genes with new functions. In addition, it is now possible to compare entire genomes—mice to human, for example. These and other comparisons show that quite different organisms have surprisingly similar genes. The wide variety of organisms is therefore the result, not so much of dissimilar genetic content as of the difference in how similar genes are used. Gene function is regulated by genetic programs—programs that control embryonic development, for example (Raff 1996).

In my view, genetic programs are analogous to musical compositions. They determine which notes are played at what time and for how long; genetic programs work similarly by organizing when, where, and for how long genes are active. How nature generates new genetic programs from the ones it produced earlier in evolution is also a matter of intense current research (Lynch and Coney 2003). Organismic complexification, however, is not obligatory. Which ones diversify and evolve into higher forms of life depends on chance and the opportunities provided by the environment. Yes, there is complexification in evolution; the process, however, is probabilistic (historic), not a fated "ascent" from lower to higher. Complexification is probabilistic, not "railroaded"; teleomorphic, not teleological (Brun 2002, 181).

The entire process is driven directly or indirectly by the energy released in the original explosion of the big bang. It is this energy that makes sequential syntheses possible. The result of syntheses, however, is the emergence of new wholes, which then may provide the elements from which new wholes may become synthesized. From this view on cosmogenesis, Karl Popper is precisely right: "We live in an universe of emergent properties" (Popper 1974, 281).

What Is Emergence?

Emergence is the universal phenomenon that synthesis brings forth new wholes with properties different from their (isolated) parts. Examples are the emergence of atoms from elementary particles, the emergence of molecules from the integration of atoms, the emergence of life from the integration of molecules, and the evolution of increasingly complex organisms from the synthesis of new genomes.

Science can trace the history of the universe and describe how it came into existence. The mechanisms can be described, their pathways analyzed and understood. Why it is, however, that synthesis brings forth new existence is, in my view, fundamentally inexplicable. I therefore respectfully disagree with Ursula Goodenough when she states, "The concept of emergence is both descriptive *and explanatory*" (2001, 204; emphasis added). I rather agree with Ernst Mayr that "more complex systems seem to resist analysis." This is because "new and previously unpredictable characters emerge at higher levels of complexity in hierarchical systems" (1982, 63-64).

The most complex hierarchical system that nature produced is the human brain. Sequential integrative steps brought forth our self-conscious mind. It emerged from anatomical and mental parts and modules of the conscious minds of our animal ancestors. Our mind, therefore, is a construct that emerged through the synthetic steps that result from the creativity of nature. Because our mind is a result of the creativity of nature, it is connected to nature. The deepest root of our mind is connected to the nature of nature. It reaches into the source of creativity and, in this way, becomes itself creative. This is why we can explore nature—create a mathematical language, for example, capable of formulating how nature works. Human creativity is a continuation of the creativity of nature. In technology and art, it is also the unification of parts that brings forth new wholes. Works of art—whether paintings, dance, or music—emerge from the integration of elements. Areas on a painting consist of unities that integrate form, color, and brush strokes. The overall composition integrates all parts into an overarching, static unity. To choreograph a dance means to integrate dynamic parts into a dynamic unity; and music emerges from the unification of notes, bars, and melodies into an overarching dynamic whole. In static and dynamic wholes, the unity transcends its parts yet only exists through the empirical reality of its parts. The constructs of nature and works of art are unities that emerge from the unification of parts that are unities themselves. The creativity of nature and human creativity bring forth hierarchies that unify elements that are hierarchies themselves. Unities, therefore, are complex because they emerge from the unification of unities that are unified complexities themselves. In nature and art, creativity brings forth unified complexity.

The structure of nature and art is simplex. Simplexity is unity in diversity, unity that transcends its parts. Transcendence and immanence are therefore not mutually exclusive but interdependent dimensions of all unities.

TRANSCENDENTALISM VERSUS EMPIRICISM: A CHOICE?

The transcendentalist in Wilson's book is of course not debating the structure of reality but rather makes the case for theism, the belief in a personal God (1998, 241). The transcendentalist's fundamental point is that there must be a creator of the universe because one cannot explain why there is something rather than nothing (p. 242).

The empiricist acknowledges that religion has an overwhelming attraction for the human mind and that religious conviction is largely beneficent. Religion rises from the innermost coil of the human spirit. It nourishes love, devotion, and above all, hope. People hunger for the assurance it offers. I can think of nothing more emotionally compelling than the Christian doctrine that incarnated himself in testimony of the sacredness of all human life, even of the slave, and that he died and rose again in promise of eternal life for everyone (p. 244).

However, hundreds of thousands of belief systems existed in human history. Many have been, and are still, used to foster ethnic wars. Christian rulers could justify aggression using passages in the Old Testament in which God himself ordered genocide (Deut. 20:16-17).

Jesus tells Pilate that he was not born to be of this world, the most dangerous of devotions (John 18:36). "With a second life waiting, suffering can be endured—especially in other people. The natural environment can be used up. Enemies of the faith can be savaged and suicidal martyrdom praised" (Wilson 1998, 245). True, all of these terrible things happened and are still happening. Jesus' statement to Pilate, however, is not the center of Christianity—Christ is. Deciding whether he is just another human invention is of course a personal decision.

CHRISTIANITY: A SYNTHESIS OF TRANSCENDENTALISM AND EMPIRICISM?

Within Christianity, there is a view relevant to the problem of immanence and transcendence. It is that God who transcends the world became immanent in the world. This is not an insight of human knowledge but a matter of faith.

Christian faith also proclaims that the world was created through the Word of God, which *is* God. This Word departed from God, was given away to creation, so that the world could become. In this view, creation is the gift of God's Word to the world. Through this gift, the world—not God—comes into being in time. The world, therefore, can be misinterpreted from the perspective of naturalism as that "which is all there is"—misinterpreted because the dimension of gift is reduced to "existence out of itself" instead of acknowledging "existence given." Religious naturalism, however, comes close to Christian perspective, to the belief that "the deeper vision we seek to attain is not of another realm or an invisible spirit but rather a revised insight into the importance of things. There is a depth not apart from but right in the midst of things" (Stone 2003, 785).

A genuine gift, a gift really given away, is unconditional, with no strings attached. A true gift also reflects the nature of the giver. Therefore, if creation is the gift of the Word of God to creation and, from the Christian perspective creation, emerges from this gift, then creation reflects the nature of God. It does so because all that exists in creation can only exist as a one. This oneness, however, is not flat and indistinct but is diversity unified into complex simplicity. In this way, creation mirrors the simplexity of the Trinitarian Creator, the simplexity of the nature of absolute existence that is One in the difference of Father, Son, and Holy Spirit. From this perspective, there is no choice to make between transcendentalism and empiricism. The task rather seems to be to train our eyes again to see and appreciate the wonder of existence. Help is available not only from the photographs taken by the Hubble Space Telescope but also from poetry "that prickles the skin!" (Wilson 1998, 247).

Note: I thank Professor C. David Grant, Department of Religion at Texas Christian University, for the critical reading of the draft of this essay.

REFERENCES

Barrow, John, and Frank Tipler. 1986. *The Anthropic Cosmological Principle.* Oxford: Clarendon, and New York: Oxford Univ. Press.
Brun, Rudolf. 2002. "Cosmology, Cosmic Evolution, and Sacramental Reality: A Christian Contribution." *Zygon: Journal of Religion and Science* 37 (March): 175-92.
Chaisson, Eric, and Steve McMillan. 1999. *Astronomy Today.* Third ed. Upper Saddle River, N.J.: Prentice-Hall.

Darwin, Charles. [1859] 1902. *The Origin of Species: By Means of Natural Selection or the Preservation of Favoured Races in the Struggle for Life.* London: John Murray.

Descartes, R. [1637] 1988. *Discourse on the Method.* In *The Philosophical Writings of Descartes.* Cambridge, London, New York: Cambridge Univ. Press.

―――. [1664] 1985. *The World and Treatise of Man.* In *The Philosophical Writings of Descartes.* Cambridge, London, New York: Cambridge Univ. Press.

Feuerbach, Ludwig. [1841] 1975. *The Essence of Christianity.* Translated from the German by George Eliot. New York: Harper and Brothers.

―――. [1851] 1967. *Lectures on the Essence of Religion.* Translated by Ralph Manheim. New York: Harper and Row.

Goodenough, Ursula. 2001. "A Setback to the Dialogue: Response to Huston Smith." *Zygon: Journal of Religion and Science* 36 (June): 201-6.

Kant, Immanuel. [1788] 1977. *Critique of Practical Reason.* Translated and edited by Mary Gregor. Cambridge and New York: Cambridge Univ. Press.

Lissauer, J. 2002. "Extrasolar Planets." *Nature* 419 (September): 355-58.

Lynch, Michael, and John S. Conery. 2003. "The Origins of Genome Complexity." *Science* 302 (November): 1401-4.

Mayr, Ernst. 1982. *The Growth of Biological Thought, Diversity, Evolution, and Inheritance.* Cambridge: Harvard Univ. Press, Belknap Press.

Overbye, Dennis. 2003. "Zillions of Universes? Or Did Ours Get Lucky?" *New York Times* (28 October). *www.nyt.com.*

Popper, Karl. 1974. *Unended Quest: An Intellectual Autobiography.* La Salle, Ill.: Open Court.

Raff, Rudolf A. 1996. *The Shape of Life: Genes, Development, and the Evolution of Animal Form.* Chicago: Univ. of Chicago Press.

Russell, Robert J. 1993. "Introduction." In *Quantum Cosmology and the Laws of Nature: Scientific Perspectives on Divine Action,* ed. Robert J. Russell, Nancey Murphy, and C. J. Isham, 1-32. Vatican City State: Vatican Observatory, and Berkeley, Calif.: Center for Theology and the Natural Sciences, dist. Univ. of Notre Dame Press.

Stone, Jerome A. 2003. "Is Nature Enough? Yes." *Zygon: Journal of Religion and Science* 38 (December): 783-800.

West, M., R. Côté, R. Marzke, and A. Jordan. 2004. "Reconstructing Galaxy History from Globular Clusters." *Nature* 427 (January): 31-35.

Wilson, Edward O. 1998. *Consilience.* New York: A. Knopf.

DOES GOD PLAY DICE?
A RESPONSE TO NIELS H. GREGERSEN,
"THE IDEA OF CREATION AND THE
THEORY OF AUTOPOIETIC PROCESSES"

(*Zygon*, vol. 34, no. 1 [March 1999])

Abstract. The idea that the Creator has a plan for creation is deeply rooted in the Christian notion of providence. This notion seems to suggest that the history of creation must be the execution of the providential plan of God. Such an understanding of divine providence expects science to confirm that cosmic history is under supernatural guidance, that evolution is therefore oriented toward a goal—to bring forth human beings, for example. The problem is, however, that science finds evidence for neither supernatural guidance nor teleology in nature. To address this problem, I understand Niels H. Gregersen to suggest that God *is* involved in the creative process. The reason science cannot demonstrate God's supernatural guidance of evolution is that the Creator structures the process from within. Gregersen argues that God is involved in the process of creation by changing the overall probability pattern of evolving systems.

In my view, such a model of how God interacts with creation is supported neither by Orthodox Christianity nor by modern science. After a critique of Gregersen's argument and a brief history of the relationship between Christianity and science, I shall suggest an alternative. It is that the freedom of creation to create itself is implicit in the fundamental dogma of Christianity that God is love.

Niels H. Gregersen points to important discoveries by modern science. The first is that chance alone, even if combined with necessity, will not create the world. Variations cannot just be haphazard but must follow rules of self-organization. Gregersen skillfully brings up the work of Stuart Kauffman, who formulated some of these mathematical rules and used them for modeling evolution (1998, 344-47).

A second fundamental insight made by science is that the past does not contain the future. Here, Gregersen discusses some important aspects of the physicist Ilya Prigogine's work (pp. 339-40). Time brings forth genuine novelty. The time of the future is open. Therefore, it is through the events that *do* happen that nature becomes what it is. Self-creation through time, self-production, or autopoiesis is indeed a central insight into how nature works. The general importance of this discovery lies in the realization that the history of nature is true history, not an unfolding of a predetermined plot.

How can theology deal with science's firm assertion that there is no teleology in evolution? Gregersen suggests that the reason science cannot find evidence of evolution following a plan is that God influences the process from within. God "not only sustains the world in general but also influences particular processes by changing the overall probability pattern of evolving systems" (abstract, p. 333). The thesis states that "God is creative by supporting and stimulating autopoietic processes" (p. 334). God binds Godself to the internal dynamics of creation (p. 348); the energy of God works inside creation (p. 350). *"We might say that the blessing of God is a structuring principle, at once transcendent in its origination and immanent in its efficiency"* (p. 352, emphasis in original). "God creates *by letting be"* (p. 353, emphasis in original), "by letting the world into existence and thereby also leaving room for a self-development of nature" (p. 353).

In section 2, titled "Short-Sighted Chance, Long-Sighted Laws," Gregersen cites the statistician David J. Bartholomew, "Since chance is such an integral part of creation, it must be part of God's plan. Thus we can agree that everything which happens is ultimately God's responsibility while denying that every single happening has a meaning in terms of God's intention. His purpose is rather to be seen in the aggregate effects of many happenings" (1984, 118). The religious interpretation of Bartholomew's statement, Gregersen suggests, is that "the distributions of chance are not arbitrary but are depending on God's initial setting. By letting the world into being as a self-organizing and even *sometimes* [emphasis mine] self-reproductive world, God is continuously upholding the self-productive capacities of matter from its simple to most complex form" (p. 355). Gregersen continues, "As creator of the self-evolving world, then God is continuously acting *a-morally* (since randomization occurs with no distinction between good and evil) but God is not acting *im-morally*, i.e. with an evil intent" (p. 355, emphasis mine). "God is seen as *reshaping the possibilities, as history goes along, by acting in different ways in different contexts"* (p. 359, emphasis in original). "[T]he dice are not only loaded once and for all but also *'differently re-loaded in the continuation of* evolutionary *history"* (p. 360, emphasis mine). "God may change the constraints themselves at many different levels . . . probability pathways are raised for some pathways rather than for others" (p. 361). "Thus, from a scientific perspective God apparently does nothing!" (p. 362). Yet "the creative reconfiguration of nature by God takes on a thoroughly temporal or processual character" (p. 362). Furthermore, "God is the creator of the fixed laws of elementary physics (a nonnegotiable position)" (p. 364 n. 21.1).

Evaluation of Gregersen's Argument: The View from Science

Modern physics discovered that the laws of nature came into being as events in the history of the universe. In earliest times, gravity, the strong force and the weak force, emerged within fractions of seconds after the big bang. Light was born about one million years later, together with electromagnetism. The evolutionary process that brought forth atoms and then molecules also brought forth the laws that govern them. The laws that control the properties of water, for example—that it can be a gas, a liquid, or a solid ice—came into existence together with the first molecules of water. In the realm of life, the law of natural selection came into existence together with the synthesis of life. This law of nature that makes its power known to any self-replicating entity did not exist before life emerged.

Charles Darwin discovered the two-step process of variation and natural selection through which plants and animals appeared. Through one long argument, Darwin convincingly showed that organisms had evolved through natural law, not supernatural intervention.

God: Artificer or Creator?

The fundamental insight of modern science that nature is capable of constructing itself is not yet fully appreciated by theology. The old image of God as the supreme artificer and designer still stands in the way of a deeper insight into the miracle of creation. The power of God is not analogous to human power, only infinitely stronger. Such an anthropocentric understanding of the power of God leads to the belief that events in the history of creation must be under supernatural control, that the world is at best only "sometimes self-reproductive" (p. 355). From our understanding of how we implement plans, we extrapolate to how God plans. In the old static model of creation, the power of the Creator united eternal forms with matter. From this unification, the substance of everything came instantly into being.

Then geologists and paleontologists discovered that the earth and its organisms were not created instantly but had changed through an enormous length of time. Some explained these changes by assuming multiple creations. Perhaps God had created multiple times, perhaps after natural disasters?

With Newton's discovery that gravity controls the movements of planets and stars, the Creator became the supreme artificer. The world was a clock that God had fine-tuned to make the world run on its own. Consequently, God did not have to interfere with the world. It was engineered in such a way that the world would work all by itself.

The skeptic David Hume objected to such an extrapolation of human creativity to the mind of the Creator "because there is a great and immeasurable, incomprehensible, difference between the *human* and the *divine* mind" ([1779] 1976, 249; emphasis in original).

Against such skepticism, William Paley argued that design in nature clearly pointed to the existence of a supreme designer. Had not a supreme engineer designed the eyes of birds to see in the air but those of fish to see in the water? Just as a watch necessarily implies that there is a watchmaker, so the adaptations of organisms to their environment is proof that there is a supreme designer. Charles Darwin showed, however, that natural law is fully capable of bringing forth the adaptations that Paley had taken as proof for supernatural design. Frederick Temple, Lord Bishop of Exeter, agreed with Darwin that organisms had evolved through natural evolution but did not believe that either life (1885, 168) or the moral law (p. 176) had so evolved. From the old essentialist, static view of creation, Temple made the step toward a new dynamic understanding of how the universe had come to be. In his view, God had ordered creation in such a way that the creative movement was predetermined (mechanistic). Temple argued that evolution shows that "design was entertained at the very beginning and impressed on every particle of created matter" (p. 235). In Temple's view, the process of creation was arranged so that the beginning (almost) contained the end of the process: God had to interfere miraculously only for the origin of life and the moral law. The Temple citation at the beginning of Gregersen's article—"God did not make the things, we may say; no, but He made them make themselves"—must be understood deterministically, not in modern indeterminate terms.

It was Henri Bergson ([1907] 1911) who got rid of the deterministic straitjacket in which the thinking about nature was constrained. Nature did not mechanistically translate the blueprint of the Creator into reality. Rather, a creative thrust (*élan vital*) launched the creative process through which nature could create itself.

For theology, the task became to integrate such process thinking into a Christian doctrine of creation. For theology in the mode of process philosophy, God continuously works within creation. In contrast to the role of God in pantheism, God in process theology is not nature but transcends it, continuously acting, however, within creation in a way that is somewhat analogous to the way the human mind acts upon the body. God (mind) is acting in the world (body) yet without being the world itself. (For variations on this theme and references, see Russell 1993.)

Orthodox Christianity has fundamental problems with process theology. The freedom of God becomes questionable because God (the mind) in process theology becomes vulnerable through what happens in the world (body). In addition, process theology affirms that God is guiding the creative process from within creation. If this is so, why does God not steer history around the Holocaust or the genocides in Bosnia, Rwanda, or Cambodia? How can the actions of God within creation remain morally neutral (amoral) if the outcome of such neutrality is catastrophe, perversity, and slaughter? Is God perhaps powerless to prevent disasters in creation? Process thought calls the omnipotence of God into question because of the grim reality of evil. This is in sharp contrast to the belief of Orthodox Christianity as expressed in the Nicene Creed. Christians believe in God the Father, the Almighty, not in a creator whose freedom is restrained by evolution. Orthodox Christianity holds that God the Father passionately loves the world, not that God acts amorally in the world. The providential plan of God is to save creation through the death and resurrection of God's son Jesus Christ, not by structuring the process of evolution. For these reasons, I cannot see how to harmonize the view expressed in "The Idea of Creation and the Theory of Autopoietic Processes" with Orthodox Christian belief as expressed in the Nicene Creed.

From the perspective of science, Gregersen builds a model of how the Creator interacts with a creation in which science has no place. If God directs evolution by throwing loaded dice, scientists cannot really understand how nature works, and their life and insights become meaningless. Given the background of the accomplishments of modern science, the suggestion that God is tampering with cosmic evolution is absurd. Einstein was precisely right, "God does not play dice."

To update the Christian doctrine of creation, one must take seriously the fundamental discovery of science that nature is fully capable of creating itself.

On the other hand, Orthodox Christianity holds that God creates and saves the world not through evolution but out of love, through God's son Jesus Christ. As I see it, an updated Christian doctrine of creation must therefore be secured by the scientific discovery that nature creates itself and, in the fundamental dogma of Christianity, that God is love.

CONSTRUCTING AN UPDATED CHRISTIAN DOCTRINE OF CREATION

An updated Christian doctrine of creation has to be anchored by Christian dogma on one side and by the scientific discovery of universal evolution on the other.

As far as I know, it was the Russian philosopher and theologian Vladimir S. Solovyev (1851-1900) who first fully appreciated the importance of Darwin's discovery for Christianity. Solovyev writes,

> Why must nature experience the pains of birth, and why, before it can generate the perfect and eternal organism, must it produce so many ugly, monstrous broods which are unable to endure the struggle for existence and perish without a trace? Why does God leave nature to reach her goals so slowly and by such ill means? Why, in general, is the realization of divine idea in the world a gradual and complex process, and not a single, simple act? The full answer to this question is contained in one word, which expresses something without which neither God nor nature can be conceived; the word is freedom. ([1873] 1948, 179)

The reason that without freedom, "neither God nor nature can be conceived" is that without freedom, there cannot be love. We know from experience that a loving relationship can only be entered into and committed to freely. In order to be able to give oneself away, one first has to become oneself. This becoming requires the freedom to create oneself through one's own history. I have to be free to become me!

As human beings, we can experience the nature of love so we can understand the revelation that the Christian God is love. Human love cannot be forced on anyone; it has to be accepted freely. The same is true for the loving relationship offered by the Creator to creation. True, the love of God surpasses all human understanding; yet without freedom, there cannot be love. Therefore creation has to be free to create itself. Without this freedom, nature could not bring forth free human beings capable of accepting or rejecting the loving relationship offered by the Creator (Brun 1994).

CREATION AND SALVATION, ETERNITY AND TIME

It is also essential to Christianity that the plan of God to save creation be real. How can God's plan of salvation be realized in a creation capable of creating itself? Before wrestling with this paradox, it might be helpful to address a related paradox: the concepts of predestination and human freedom. According to Christian revelation, human beings freely realize through living what they are predestined to do from eternity (see Rom. 9:28-30; Eph. 1:41-4). Could these paradoxical situations be a consequence of the relationship between eternity and time? I think it is essential to search for an answer to this question. Saint Augustine, for example, writes,

> It is not with God as it is with us. He does not look ahead to the future, look directly at the present, look back to the past. He sees in some manner, utterly remote from anything we experience or could imagine. He does not see things by turning his attention from one thing to another. He sees all without any kind of change. Things which happen under the condition of time are in the future, not yet in being, or in the present, already existing, or in the past, no longer being. But God comprehends all these in a stable and eternal present . . . . His knowledge is not like ours, which has three tenses: present, past and future. God's knowledge has no change or variation. ([ca. 400] 1972, 452)

Furthermore, in Saint Augustine's *Confessions*, we read, "Just as you knew heaven and earth in the beginning without that bringing any variation into your knowing, so you made heaven and earth in the beginning without that meaning a tension between past and future in your activity" ([ca. 400] 1991, 254).

Saint Augustine concluded that God does not create sequentially in time but in one eternal, creative act. God is the Prime Mover who does not move—for movement is in time, God is not. In the words of Saint Thomas, God creates the world *sine motu, ex nihilo* (without motion, out of nothing).

More recently, Karl Barth formulated some of his insights into the relationship between time and eternity: "Time is distinguished from eternity by the fact that in it beginning, middle and end are distinct and even opposed as past, present, and future" (1957, 608). "Eternity is pure duration and in this duration *God is free*" (1957, 609; emphasis mine). "What distinguishes eternity from time is the fact that there is in Him no opposition or competition or conflict but peace between origin, movement and goal, between present, past and the future, between 'not yet,' 'now,' and 'no more,' between rest and movement, potentiality and actuality, whither and whence, here and there, this and that" (1957, 612). What is in time separated into past, present, and future, for God is integrated into the oneness of pure, eternal duration.

This way of thinking about the relationship that exists between eternity and time might reveal how creation can fulfill God's plan by creating itself freely. Such a concept is beyond human understanding. I think, however, that we can understand that we cannot understand. The reflection upon the relationship between eternity and time also sheds light on the paradox of predestination and free will. For Christianity, the passion of Jesus Christ is the most powerful example that eternal determination and free will are not mutually exclusive. Here, everyone, including Judas, is acting freely—yet through the free actions of all involved, the saving plan of God becomes precisely executed.

From this center of Christian faith, it becomes clear that the paradox that exists between predestination and human freedom has to be left standing. It is one aspect of the belief in God Almighty. Analogously, it is in God's power to create creation that can create itself. Yet by doing so, the plan of God for creation becomes precisely executed. But where and when?

Almighty God intervenes in the history of creation through the life, death, and resurrection of Jesus Christ. In this moment of time, the eternal saving act of God intersects with the history of creation. In Jesus Christ, the plan of God is realized for the past, the present, and the future because in Godman the Christ, eternity and time are one.

The presence of salvation within time does not mean, however, that the world is not the world anymore. Salvation is within the world, offered to the world, but it does not destroy the freedom of the world. The world remains the same except that at each point in history, salvation is freely offered in Jesus Christ. In good times as well as in the experience of evil, in every moment of each human life, salvation is extended in the invitation to walk with Christ. It is in following him that we human beings, who represent the world, are honored to contribute to salvation too. "For creation waits with eager expectation the revelation of the children of God" (Rom. 8:19). The children of God are not taken out of this world but are sent into the world. This mission does not preclude the possibility of evil, but it includes the promise that "God will wipe every tear from our eyes" (Rev. 7:17).

Conclusion

To find the rightful place for the history of the universe within Christian theology, I suggest separating the history of creation from the history of salvation. The two are separate because the history of creation continues into an open future, whereas the history of salvation ends in Jesus Christ. The point is that eternity and time are neither congruent nor parallel but are, so to speak, perpendicular to one another. Linear time, the time of history, runs from beginning to end. Eternity, however, transcends time yet is present within each moment.

The connection between God and nature is the unity of God and humanity, eternity and time, in Jesus Christ. He is the gift of God to creation. Christ is the Word of God that departs from God, emptying himself so that creation can create itself through him and in him (Col. 1:16). In Christ, creation is created *and* saved.

Without freedom on both sides, the loving relationship offered by the Creator to creation would be impossible. The scientific discovery that nature is capable of freely creating itself makes explicit what is already implicated in the fundamental dogma of Christianity—that God is love.

References

Aquinas, Saint Thomas. [ca. 1270] 1964. *Summa Theologiae.* Ia, 45, I. New York: McGraw-Hill, Blackfriars Press.

Augustine. [ca. 400] 1972. *The City of God.* Trans. Henry Bettenson, Ltd. Harmondsworth, Middlesex, England: Penguin.

———. [ca. 400] 1991. Confessions. Trans. Henry Chadwick. Oxford: Oxford Univ. Press.

Barth, Karl. 1957. *Church Dogmatics: The Doctrine of God.* Vol. 2, first half-volume. Harold Knight, trans. (pp. 297-439). Edinburgh: T. and T. Clark.

Bartholomew, David J. 1984. *God of Chance.* London: SCM Press.

Bergson, Henri. [1907] 1911. *Creative Evolution.* New York: H. Holt.

Brun, Rudolf B. 1994. "Integrating Evolution: A Contribution to the Christian Doctrine of Creation." *Zygon: Journal of Religion and Science* 29 (September): 275-96.

Gregersen, Niels Henrik. 1998. "The Idea of Creation and the Theory of Autopoietic Processes." *Zygon* 33 (September): 333-67.

Hume, David. [1779] 1976. *Dialogues Concerning Natural Religion*. Oxford: Clarendon Press.

Russell, Robert J. 1993. "Introduction." In *Quantum Cosmology and the Laws of Nature*, ed. R. J. Russell, N. Murphy, and C. J. Isham. Vatican City State: Vatican Observatory Press, and Notre Dame, Ind.: Univ. of Notre Dame Press.

Solovyev, Vladimir S. [1873] 1948. *Lectures on Godmanhood*. London: Dennis Dobson.

Temple, Frederick. 1885. *The Relations between Religion and Science*. London: Macmillan.

PRINCIPLES OF MORPHOGENESIS IN EMBRYONIC DEVELOPMENT, MUSIC, AND EVOLUTION

Communio, vol. 20, no. 3 [Fall 1993])

ABSTRACT   In both organismic morphogenesis and the performance of a piece of music, there is emergence of novelty through creative translation.

In this paper I propose to scrutinize the thought that organismic development and the performance of a piece of music might follow similar principles of morphogenesis. First, I will briefly summarize some insights into how organisms develop. The rationale for attempting this will be to show that there is an important difference between the genetic instructions provided by the genome of embryos on one hand, and the morphogenetic process of actual embryogenesis on the other. I will argue that embryogenesis is the result of a process of synthetic interaction between genetic and non-genetic (epigenetic) information. Both types of information have to interact with one another to create a new organism. Embryogenesis, therefore, is not just an extension of genetics but requires translation of both genetic and epigenetic information. This dynamic interaction is creative. It leads to the emergence of a new third, namely, the developing embryo.

I will then move on to music. I will argue that the performance of a piece of music, analogous to embryogenesis, is also a creative event. It is not sufficient to play the score note for note: the music has to be re-created. This creative event is dependent upon the interplay between a composition and the quality of the musicians. It is this interplay between two levels of musical organization that are essentially different from one another that creates the music. Embryogenesis and the performance of music each emerge as a new third from the interaction between two different types of information. The emergence of novelty through the interaction of different types of information will be called "creative translation."

After defining this term, I will move on to the third part of this essay in which the evolution of complex genomes will be compared to the history of polyphonic music. The rationale is to show that the analogy between organismic morphogenesis and music might also hold in the patterns of their history.

I. Embryonic development

Around the turn of the century, it had become quite clear that embryogenesis was controlled by genes. The molecular tools to analyze the molecular architecture of genetic programs that control embryonic development, however, became available only during the last twenty years or so. One surprising finding is that the quantity of genetic materials in the DNA is not strictly related to the morphological complexity of organisms. Snails contain as much DNA as mammals; salamanders might have ten times more genetic material than human beings. It is probably safe to conclude that the complexity of an organism does not so much depend on how much DNA it has, but on how its genetic material is organized. As Frank Ruddle, a leading geneticist at Yale University, recently stated: "Very much suggests that the genome is not just a bag of genes that you can shake up and rattle around." [1]

Indeed, it has become quite obvious that genes are entities integrated into genetic hierarchies. Genes positioned at high levels control the activities of several genes at lower levels of the genetic construction. These secondary genes regulate the activity of genes at still lower levels. In the fruit fly *Drosophila* for example, primary regulatory genes produce products that are necessary for the activation of secondary regulatory genes. Once these are turned on, new groups of tertiary genes are activated. These are then finally used to produce those proteins that serve as the actual building materials of the embryo. [2]

---

[1]   "Homeobox Genes Go Evolutionary," *Research News Science* 225 (1992): 399-401. For a review on Homeobox genes see: Mai Har Sham, Stefan Nonchev, Jenny Whiting, Nancy Papalopulu, Heather Marshall, Paul Hunt, Ian Muchamore, Martyn Cook, and Robb Krumlauf, "Hox-2: Gene Regulation and Segmental Patterning in the Vertebrate Head," in *Cell-Cell-Interactions in Early Development, 49th Symposium of the Society for Developmental Biology*, ed. by John Gerhart (New York: John Wiley and Sons, Inc., 1991), 129-43.

[2]   P. W. Ingham, "The Molecular Genetics of Embryonic Pattern Formation in *Drosophila,*" *Nature* (1988): 25-34.

Through direct or indirect feedback loops, gene products of regulatory genes might control their own state of activity as well as the function of other genes. In this way, lines of communications are established that allow genes to influence each other's state of activity. In short, the genes in an organism are not independent, isolated entities but are integrated into genetic networks: genes form genomes. They function as integrated, physiological units, not as bags containing genes totally independent from one another. Furthermore, genetic networks integrate gene activity in two ways. They provide chronological information necessary for pacing embryonic development, and they also control the spatial differentiation in the embryo.

The timing of embryogenesis is accomplished in at least two different ways. First, there are specialized pacemaker genes that play an important role in making "decisions"—for example, deciding at what time in embryogenesis the limbs grow out.[3] In addition, timing is also controlled by the hierarchical organization of the genome. Primary genes are activated first, and the resulting gene products turn on secondary regulatory genes later. As these are turned on, tertiary genes will become active, activating regulatory genes that are located even further down stream (as well as activating structural genes that are used to synthesize the proteins that actually build the embryo). Obviously, the synthesis of gene products takes time. This causes a delay between the activation of genes at lower and lower levels. In an approximation, one might compare this situation with a dried-out riverbed in which the water from a rainstorm in the mountains will reach lower and lower areas later and later.

This model of genetic information flowing like a cascading river from the top to the bottom of a riverbed is, however, only a first approximation. The architecture of a genome is more complicated. For example, the activation of a gene downstream might influence gene activity upstream. In addition, the effect of a recently activated gene might influence the state of other genes locally, or might propagate throughout the network.

But although the internal organization of the genome of any organism is highly complex, no organism is preformed in its genes. Rather the information stored in the genome, or the genotype, has to be translated into the actually

---

[3]   See for example: Pere Alberch, "Evolution of Developmental Processes: Irreversibility and Redundancy in Amphibian Metamorphosis," in *Development as an Evolutionary Process* (Alan R. Liss, Inc., 1987), 23-46; James Hanken, "Development and Evolution in Amphibians," *American Scientist 77* (1989): 336-43.

differentiating organism, or the phenotype. To accomplish this process, each cell of the embryo obtains a complete set of the total genetic information. However, different cells use different parts of it. Which subset of the total genetic information is actually translated in the first few cells of the early embryo depends upon the area of the fertilized egg from which these primary cells originated. In addition, heterogeneity between the cells is also generated by the sequence from which they originated from one another by successive cell divisions. Both spatial and chronological origin generates unique cellular histories.

It is essential to see that these unique cellular histories depend on the participation of the genetic information, but are not controlled by the genome. The diverse cellular histories are the result of a process that requires the interplay between epigenetic information, such as the topographical origin of the cells, their differential cytoplasmic information, and the dynamic patterns of cell divisions. These epigenetic differences unlock different subsets of information from the total genetic program. It is the interaction between the unique history of each cell on one hand, and the genetic program on the other, that creates the embryo. Therefore, embryogenesis is not just execution of a genetic program. Embryogenesis depends upon the dynamic interaction between the genetic and the epigenetic levels of organization. For example, the activation of a specific set of instructions in a particular cell leads to the production of new molecules in this cell. The presence of these newly synthesized compounds might make it possible to access new genetic information in the program. This process leads to more pronounced secondary differences between the cells. As cellular differences become more and more pronounced, the conditions within the cells change in such a way that tertiary information, also stored in the genome, becomes available. This is a second example to illustrate that without the actual creation of various cell types in the developing embryo, its genetic program cannot work.

In principle, the building of various embryonic environments is a necessary condition to activate further content of the genetic program. The genetic information necessary to further specify diversity of the embryonic organs and tissues becomes available only in this way. The process might lead to the generation of molecules that the cells secrete into their extra cellular environment. As different groups of cells secrete different types of such extra cellular compounds, a multitude of chemically well-defined microenvironments emerge within the embryo. These local environments provide the various keys necessary to open the next access to further genetic information. The resulting increased precision in the definition of the various local environments is then used for the proper differentiation of the tissues in the different organs, such as the liver, the kidney, or the brain. The point is that the genetic information has to be translated into structures that contain not genetic, but epigenetic information. It is this epigenetic information that, in a further step, is capable of accessing new genetic instructions. There has to be an interplay between what has already been built and the program. Without this translation from the genetic to the epigenetic level, without the interaction of these two different levels, organic morphogenesis is impossible. This dynamic interaction is creative because the embryo does not exist—is not somehow pre-formed—either genetically or epigenetically. The Nobel Laureate Gerald Edelman formulates this important point this way: "The expression of the appropriate developmentally important genes is epigenetic and place-dependent, relying on previously formed tissue structures."[4]

The principles that organize genes into genetic programs on the one hand, and those that are involved in the construction of the differentiating embryo on the other, are essentially different. The embryo emerges as a third new entity out of the dynamic interaction between these two different levels of organization. Organisms are not "pre-formed" at the molecular level: Squirrels can run around and bury nuts, their genetic programs cannot!

Genetic information therefore is necessary but not sufficient for embryogenesis. The examples given above illustrate that the genetic level provides only the base of a hierarchical construction that depends on the dynamic interaction with entities such as tissues and cells which are not part of the genetic base. Embryogenesis has to be understood as the emergence of a new dynamic unity brought about by the dynamic interaction of genetic as well as of epigenetic information. The total information necessary for the formation of the next step in embryogenesis is present only in the just realized embryonic stage, not in any subdivision of the genetic program alone. This is to emphasize that the embryo, at each stage of development, is a dynamic whole that cannot be adequately described by genetics alone. It is the whole dynamic system that contains the information to build itself. This is to say that this dynamic whole has properties that neither the genetic nor the epigenetic information contains.

The acknowledgement of this phenomenon of emergence, namely that the whole has qualities that the parts do not have, is neither vitalism nor

---

[4]   Gerald M. Edelman, "Morphoregulation," *Developmental Dynamics* 193 (1992): 2-10.

murky metaphysics: it is the result of rigorous reductionistic research.[5] This research has shown that embryogenesis is a process brought about by the interaction of various different levels of a hierarchically organized, dynamic unity. Epigenetic and genetic information have to interact with one another in order to bring forth a third new entity. This is to say that their information has to be translated onto a new level which is not contained by either. And so, because the interaction between genetic and epigenetic information creates the new reality of the forming organism, the translation is creative.

Creative translation is defined as the process through which a higher level of reality emerges from information at lower levels. By higher level of organization I understand the emergence of a level with properties, not present at the lower level of the elements, from which it is synthesized. Examples for the phenomenon of creative translation are: the emergence of matter from energy, the synthesis of atoms from nuclear particles, the synthesis of molecules from atoms, the emergence of life from molecules, and speciation through organismic evolution, including the emergence of human beings.

Creative translation yields a hierarchically organized universe. The integration of elements into new unities, however, does not destroy the peculiarities of the integrated elements. Integration does not mean homogenization. Rather, it is precisely through the diversity and particular property of each element that novelty may emerge through integration. The newly created unity is unity in diversity, not homogeneity. The analogy

---

5   Ernst Mayr, in his book *The Growth of Biological Thought, Diversity, Evolution and Inheritance* (Cambridge, MA: The Belknap Press of Harvard University Press, 1982), 64, discusses the phenomenon of emergence in the following way: "Two false claims against emergentism must be rejected. The first is that emergentists are vitalists. This claim, indeed, was valid for some of the nineteenth century and early twentieth century emergentists, but it is not valid for modern emergentists, who accept constitutive reduction without reservation and are therefore by definition, nonvitalists. The second is the assertion that it is part of emergentism to believe that organisms can only be studied as wholes, and that any further analysis is to be rejected. Perhaps there have been holists who have made such a claim, but this view is certainly alien to 99 percent of all emergentists. All they claim is that explanatory reduction is incomplete, since new and previously unpredictable characters emerge at higher levels of complexity in hierarchical systems. Hence complex systems must be studied at every level, because each level has properties not shown at lower levels."

between embryogenesis and the performance of a piece of music is based on this view.

II. Morphogenesis in music

The origin of music is difficult to trace. Who can tell how a musical idea, Mozart's "Jupiter Symphony" for example, comes to be? Obviously, the work of a composer is essentially creative work. Since I am not a composer, I can only vaguely suggest that composing music might essentially be integrative work. This is to say that a musical idea has to become integrated into the elements of a musical form—it has to be written into notes on paper. A musical idea has to become incarnated into symbols, translated into a musical score. This translation is creative because the idea becomes reality through its expression in its musical form. Susanne Langer writes:

"The musician, of course, is making a piece of music. Now music is something audible, as a picture is something visible, not merely in conception but in sensible existence. When a piece of music is completely made, it is there to be heard by the physical as well as the inward ear . . . . A musician may sit at the keyboard, putting all sorts of themes and figures together in a loose fantasy, until one idea takes over and a structure emerges from the wandering sounds; or he may hear, all at once, without the distinction of any physical tones, perhaps even without exact tone color as yet, the whole musical apparition. But however the total *Gestalt* presents itself to him, he recognizes it as the fundamental form of the piece; and henceforth his mind is no longer free to wander irresponsibly from theme to theme, key to key, and mood to mood. This form is the "composition" which he feels called upon to develop."[6]

In human creativity the synthetic process oscillates between the expression of an idea into the adequate form on the one hand, and the emerging form and the original idea on the other. It is the initial idea in the mind of the composer that starts the creative process. But as the idea comes to be, the reality of this emerging form interacts with it. A dispute between the idea and its form begins, a dispute that searches for the correct expression, for the unity in which they may become one. It is this oneness that emerges as novelty from the integration of idea and form. Neither idea nor form contain the reality

---

[6]   Susanne K. Langer, *Feeling and Form: A Theory of Art* (New York: Charles Scribners, 1953), 120-21.

that emerges from the form that expresses the idea. The synthesis of form and idea creates novelty, namely, the new reality of the expressed idea. The perhaps somewhat extreme case of Ludwig van Beethoven might illustrate the point. Donald Grout writes: "Beethoven kept notebooks in which he jotted down plans and themes for compositions, and thanks to these sketchbooks we can sometimes follow the progress of a musical idea through various stages until it reaches its final form."[7]

From this perspective, composing music might be understood as creative translation from the top down, from the idea into notes. This is the content of the concept of creative translation in music, the novelty that emerges from the translation of the idea into its adequate form. This primary creative event, however, is not complete in itself. The musical work of a composer has to be performed in order to complete the primary creative act.

I shall now try to unfold the suggested analogy between embryogenesis and the performance of a piece of music. This part of the argument is moving away from the discussion of the primary creative act of composing music. Instead, it will focus on the extension of this primary creative act into the analysis of the nature of a musical performance. The essence of the argument will be that the performance of music is dependent upon the creative interaction between the musical score and the musicians who perform the work. Analogous to the emergence of the embryo through the synthetic interaction between genetic and epigenetic information, a musical performance has to emerge through its re-creation. The notes on paper and the musical information that skilled musicians bring with them through their talent and training have to dynamically interact in order to resurrect the music. Analogous to the way in which genetic programs provide the information for embryonic differentiation, so too do the musical symbols on a sheet of paper provide the instructions for the performance of a piece of music. But as the conductor gives the sign to enter into the realm of music, the inky symbols in their paper grave have to be brought back to musical life.

Obviously, the written composition guides the performance of a piece of music. Maybe the cellos first create a musical environment into which the violins can enter. And as they translate their part from the notes, they might start talking to the bases. This dialogue might then provide the correct space in which the flutes can carry on. Analogous to differentiating embryonic cells that have to interact with one another in order to create the correct environment

---

[7]   Donald J. Grout, *A History of Western Music* (New York: W. W. Norton, 1973), 514.

in which further action can take place, so the performance of a piece of music has to create the musical space into which the music can emerge.

Just as organisms are not pre-formed in their genetic programs, so the performance of a piece of music is not encapsulated in a composition. First, a note has not just to be played but created. The sound produced has to express the spiritual realm of music before it can be integrated into the musical idea of a particular piece. This is a basic requirement because sound is the primary element of music. The various sounds are integrated into patterns that are themselves integrated into higher musical structures. A piece of music is an integrated, hierarchically organized structure. This hierarchy cannot be musical if its primary element, the sound produced, is not.[8] Harmony, melody, timber, and phrasing all depend on the primary spirituality of the sound. That spirit is not in the written notes, but has to be re-created through the sound that emerges out of the musical spirit of the performer. The performance of a piece of music has to re-create the musical idea of the composer. This can happen only if the performance re-creates the musical form, in which that idea can again become concrete. Therefore, the composer's idea expressed on paper has to be creatively translated back into musical life, not just mechanically played. In order to accomplish this creative task, the musicians in the orchestra have to lend their musical spirit to the work. They have to become one with the musical idea so that it can again become real through its incarnation into its form. The musical idea has to be creatively translated into its form.

Creative translation occurs at different levels. As already argued above, the incarnation of the musical idea into musical form is the first creative translation accomplished by the composer. Once the music is written down on paper, a second type of creative translation has to take place, namely, the translation of the score into an actual performance. This secondary type of creative translation continues the creative process that started with the composer. Performance now is service—creative service that lends the spirit of the performer to the work and, in this way, brings it back to life. Performance

---

[8]   Miles Davis comes to my mind: what an incredible expression the sound of his trumpet had in every note. And of course all the great jazz musicians exhibit the same phenomenon, from Louis Armstrong to Stan Getz and Jerry Mulligan, to name just a few. Yet not only the sound of individual instrumentalists, but entire orchestras can be expressive: the sound that Duke Ellington's orchestra created carried a message, a message from his soul.

is service because what is resurrected through the spirit of the performer is primarily the work of the composer, not the work of the performer. A piece of music, a fugue of Bach, measure by measure constructs itself.

Genes and notes are different elements, of course. The principles involved in the creative translation of genetic and epigenetic information into a new organism, however, or the necessary interplay between a composition and the musicians that re-create it during a performance, is the same. Embryogenesis and music manifest one and the same creative principle of dynamic architecture. The performance of a piece of music follows the same principle of organismic morphogenesis. In both cases there is emergence of novelty through creative translation.

What is the nature of this creative process? In a first approach I shall suggest that both embryos and musical performances construct themselves through sequential diversification. Embryonic differentiation is accomplished by sequential diversification into differing embryonic parts. It is the construction of a more and more differentiated organismic whole by more and more precise distinctions between its parts. Embryogenesis is the dynamic construction of more and more distinct unity by differentiating into more and more distinct diversity.

This might be the fundamental principle in music too. Already, a tone is constructed in this way. The regularity of its vibrations distinguishes it from noise. It also gives a tone a fixed pitch. A tone, therefore, is a unity that emerges out of the regularity of its vibrations. One and the same tone can have a different timber or color, depending on whether it is played by a trumpet or a violin. This is an example of unity in diversity at a new level, namely that a tone, which is already an integrated unit, can be different, yet remain the same.

Unity in diversity is also the structure of an even more complex musical element, the chord. The basic tone, its octave fifth and fourth played together, forms a new musical structure. This unity of a chord can be so strong that it is difficult to hear its parts, namely, the notes from which it emerges. It was Pythagoras and his students who discovered the interesting fact that a stretched string, divided in 1/2, 2/3, 3/4, etc. and plucked, produced the octave, the fifth and the fourth. This shows that the four notes are interrelated. The length of one and the same string, subdivided in simple different proportions, produces distinctly different tones. Yet, played together they manifest their unity in the difference of the one emerging chord. The chord is a musical unity that shows integration at a higher level than the level of a simple tone. The quality of the chord is distinctly new, but totally dependent on the integrated diversity of its individual components. And, perhaps most surprisingly, this newly synthesized whole can be integrated into still higher structures, without losing its identity. Chords can serve as elements in a higher order structure as they are played sequentially. Chopin's "Marche Funébre" comes to mind. It is dynamic unity that may emerge out of the diversity of sequentially arranged chords. To come back to the suggested analogy between organisms and music, any organ in an organism is a unified diversity of cell types, and any organism is an integrated dynamic whole of all its parts. Although the building material in music is tones and in organisms is cells, the principle of morphogenesis is the same. It is to create a dynamic unity through sequential diversification of elements.

In organogenesis as well as in music, the dynamic construction is accomplished through hierarchically organized, spatio-temporal elements. These are integrated entities themselves that emerged from the synthesis of elements at still lower levels.

III. The history of polyphonic music, and genetic principles of organismic evolution

Although the Greeks discovered chords, as far as I know they did not use them in their musical constructions. Perhaps, their compositions were rather similar to Eastern music, in which the musical construction develops strictly linearly, without the vertical components of chords. This serial construction of musical architecture is based on dynamic foundations. These are provided by strict rules that allow dynamic unity to emerge from integrated linearity, without breaking up into unrelated, linear pieces.

During the early Middle Ages, the music of the West was also exclusively serially constructed. Gregorian chant sung in support of church services was strictly linear, without any vertical harmonic support. Then an exact copy of the melody was added. It was sung simultaneously with the original melody but at a defined distance: either at the fourth or the fifth. Later, a new type of musical composition emerged, in which the original melody might have been sung together with its exact reversal. This yielded a vertical, harmonic structure that produced consonants and dissonants. And since there is a strong inborn natural desire to release the musical tensions of a dissonance into a consonance, a new, crucial, vertical principle that could be developed horizontally was discovered.

By the thirteen century, the innovation of a new interval of harmony became popular. Now, rather than the usual intervals of quints and quarts, composers frequently added thirds into their compositions. This created a new and quite different-sounding, sweeter music. It sounded much less harsh than the interval of the fifth or the quart. The discovery of the third greatly enriched the vertical as well as the horizontal possibilities of composing music. Then, during the Renaissance, composers discovered the possibility of increasing the degree of polyphonic diversity by doubling the structure of compositions that were already polyphonic units. This opened the possibility of adding instruments to support and develop melodies already sung in harmony.

In short, the history of polyphonic music shows that, in a first step, a second identical melody was added to the original one. From there, one of the two identical melodies could vary—become symmetrically reversed for example—without destroying the original melodic line. However, the presence of a similar melody sung at the same time as the original one created new musical elements that interacted with one another. The process continued with the doubling of existing musical structures, which then allowed these to diversify without jeopardizing the original construction. This new diversification became possible under the protection of the basic melodic line. These already complex compositions could further increase in complexity by doubling the already doubled structures again. Thus, out of the monophonic Gregorian chant, polyphonic music had emerged.

Interestingly, the manner in which single melodic lines evolved into complex polyphonic patterns seems to have followed a principle of morphogenesis that also led to increasing genetic complexity during organismic evolution. Here too, the process started most likely with a single line of genetic information capable of reproducing itself. At some point in time a situation evolved in which two identical strings did not separate from one another but propagated first as two identical copies. This made it possible for one string of information to change by spontaneous chemical alterations (mutations), while the other assured survival by still executing the original function. Then a situation might have emerged in which the doubled string doubled again. Doubling of genes allowed mutations to further accumulate in redundant regions as long as at least one set of genes ascertained the reproduction of the complex.[9] Repetition of genetic motifs allowed the occurrence of mutations in these first identical elements. This introduced variations into the genetic system, which probably did not have any functions at first. But mutations generated connections between the old and the new mutated strings of information.

---

[9]   For details, see S. Ohno, *Evolution by Gene Duplication* (Berlin: J. Springer, 1970).

This allowed communication between the original set of genes and the new genes, a situation that provided additional options to respond more efficiently to fluctuations in the environment. Essentially, simple genetic systems evolved into complex ones by repeating this double step process time and time again.

If the complexity of any system increases beyond a certain tolerable level, it will very likely degenerate. If the argument here presented of ever-increasing complexity—from the original explosion to the emergence of the human mind—is correct, how did nature manage to escape disaster? First, time and time again, disaster did strike: complex systems degenerated frequently. The dying out of over 90% of all species that ever lived on earth might have been due, at least in part, to genetic systems that became too complex to function.

Similarly, in music, the predominating styles of composition had to be broken up time and time again in order to escape what had become a lifeless stiffness of the old styles. Periods of chaotic oscillations and quests for new ways to compose were frequent. Ultimately, new styles were synthesized from the pieces left over after musical revolutions. In short, the analogy between organismic evolution and the history of music can be made from this perspective too.

In spite of the constraint imposed by complexity, increasingly complex systems did emerge in nature. How did nature increase complexity, from atoms to the human brain, in spite of the disastrous fate that looms in complexity? One way was to duplicate structures. This made complex structures less vulnerable, because if one complex element did not function, a second one perhaps still worked. But a second way might be perhaps more revealing if the terms "simple" and "complex" are defined.

There are two aspects of simplicity. The first is simplicity in the sense of being homogeneous, or not differentiated. In this sense a nuclear particle, a proton for example, might be declared to be simple. It follows from this point of view that an atom of hydrogen is more complex, because it is a unit that consists of a proton and an electron. If hydrogen and oxygen are synthesized into a water molecule, then obviously such a molecule is more complex than either of its atoms. Interestingly, a water molecule, although quite complex in its structure, is simple again as a water molecule: it can interact to form liquid water or become integrated in countless new and rather complex molecules. The point is that complexity at one level of organization becomes simple again at the next higher level. Complexity is not lost, but is not manifest at the new level. Here, complexity has become simple again. This means that what is complex at a lower level of organization is simple again at the higher level: nature is hierarchically organized. One expression of this hierarchical structure is the ubiquitous experience that what is simple on one level might be quite complex at the next lower level. This is the experience of all natural sciences, but especially the experience of an electron microscopist, who investigates the complexity of the elements of a "simple" cell. However not only structures of nature, but especially biological entities, are structured hierarchically.

As explained already above, hierarchical organization is also an essential aspect in music. Leonard Meyer writes:

> "Hierarchic structures are of single importance because they enable the composer to invent and the listener to comprehend complex interactive musical relationships. If musical stimuli (pitches, durations, timbres, etc.) did not form brief, but partially completed events (motives, phrases, etc.) and if these did not in turn combine with one another to form more extended, higher-order patterns, all relationships would be local and transient in the note-to-note foreground. Nonhierarchical music—that of John Cage, for instance—moves, like the ocean, in undulating or sporadic waves of activity in which we attend to, but can scarcely remember, the particular events . . . . And this is especially important in the understanding of music, which, because it is abstract and successive in time, places extraordinary demands upon memory."[10]

Patterns in nature as well as patterns in music are hierarchically organized. What is simple at high levels of the hierarchy is complex at lower levels. This is so because, in nature as well as in music, integration of the diverse creates an integrated and therefore simple unit at the higher, emergent level. This is the true integrated simplicity with which my dog catches the airborne frisbee. His attention is on the flying object, not on the nervous system that somehow has to calculate the trajectory of the airborne plastic disc, nor is it occupied with muscle movements. All these activities are integrated into the overall "simple" sequence of "just catching it."

That hierarchically organized complexity results in simplicity is also a basic phenomenon in art. It is a simplicity that emerges from the integration of the

---

[10]   Leonard B. Meyer, *Explaining Music: Essays and Explorations* (Berkeley, CA and London: University of California Press, 1973), 80.

complex. True art is not simplistic, unintegrated sameness. Rather, simplicity in art results from the idea that is integrated in the diversity of the various elements of its form. This can even take on the simplicity of integrating the mutually exclusive. In a good painting as well as in a profound musical composition, simplicity is integrated diversity.

In his essay entitled: "Toward a Theory of Profundity in Music," David E. White analyzes the pattern of Beethoven's Opus 131.[11] He writes:

> "The principal example of expressiveness in this work has been sadness, primarily as found in the first movement. But, as already noted, the same type of somberness is expressed in the fourth and the seventh movements. Thus, movements one, four and seven are identical in expressing sadness; pathos and gloom but they are, formally, quite different movements. The relevant metaphysical concern applicable to this complex pattern is that of identity and difference."[12]

The objects of nature as well as good art are hierarchically organized. In both cases, simplicity escapes the looming disaster of disintegrating complexity by unifying diversity into genuine simplicity.

In conclusion, therefore, the reason that there is an analogy between embryogenesis and music is that both reflect this fundamental principle of cosmic construction, namely, that synthesis creates novelty. Therefore, when listening to music one experiences this fundamental principle, which brought forth not only animals and plants but also every thing that, is. But why it is that synthesis creates, I do not know—I can only wonder!

---

[11]   David A. White, "Towards a Theory of Profundity in Music," *The Journal of Aesthetics and Art Criticism* 50 (1992): 31-32.

[12]   For a discussion of profundity in music see also Philip Alperson, "The Arts of Music," *The Journal of Aesthetics and Art Criticism* 50 (1992): 224.

COSMOLOGY, COSMIC EVOLUTION, AND SACRAMENTAL REALITY: A CHRISTIAN CONTRIBUTION

(*Zygon*, vol. 37, no. 1 [March 2002])

Abstract. From the Christian perspective, creation exists through the Word of God. The Word of God does not create God again but brings forth the absolute "otherness" of God: creation. The nature of God is to exist. God *is* existence as unity in the diversity of God the Father, the Son, and the Holy Spirit. The gift of created existence reflects the triune nature of the Word of God. It is synthesis of diversity into unity that creates. Nature brings forth new existence by unifying what it already brought forth previously. Therefore, the creative process of nature is self-similar and nonlinear: self-similar because at all levels it is synthesis that brings forth novelty; nonlinear because the properties of the new unities are not present in their (isolated) elements. The new properties of the wholes, however, do not destroy the properties of the parts. Rather, the elements integrated into new wholes become creatively transformed. This is because the parts become carriers of the whole, which transforms the parts through its presence. The parts become and express the qualities of the whole, qualities that the parts do not possess in isolation. Synthesis, therefore, transforms the parts creatively because synthesis is creative. The qualities of the parts become "elevated" because the whole becomes present in and through the parts. The understanding of creation as the result of sequential, creative transformations offers a glance into the mystery of the Word of God present in the Eucharist. Here, too, the elements of bread and wine are not destroyed but elevated, creatively transformed into the Word of God. The elements (bread and wine) become the carrier of a transcendent "quality," the Word of God. From this perspective, creation and the sacrament of the Eucharist illuminate each other. This is because the Word of God that creates the otherness of creation and the Word of God present in the Eucharist is the same.

GOD AND NATURE

Within the Judeo-Christian context, there are fundamental revealed insights that cannot be ignored. The biblical revelation of the relationship that exists between God and creation, for example, is unambiguous: creation is dependent on God, but God is not dependent on creation. This understanding of how God relates to creation excludes any dependency of God on creation: God *is* absolute, independent existence.[1] The biblical revelation of how God relates to creation can therefore not follow a pantheistic or a panentheistic path. It is fundamental for this view that the way God "is" and the way creation is are totally different. One aspect of this absolute difference is that God is eternal, whereas creation is in time. This is not to say that there is no relationship between God and creation. Christian revelation about this relationship makes it clear only that God is not in any way dependent upon creation. God creates creation not out of necessity but out of nothing, in absolute freedom, out of love. How the loving eternal God relates to time is a central theme for Christian thought. Augustine, for example, writes the following about this relationship between eternity and time:

> It is not with God as it is with us. He does not look ahead to the future, look directly at the present, look back to the past. He sees in some manner, utterly remote from anything we experience or could imagine. He does not see things by turning his attention from one thing to another. He sees all without any kind of change. Things, which happen under the condition of time, are in the future, not yet in being, or in the present, already existing, or in the past, no longer being. But God comprehends all these in a stable and eternal present . . . . His knowledge is not like ours, which has three tenses: present, past and future. God's knowledge has no change or variation. ([ca. 400] 1972, 452)

And in his work *Confessions*, he writes, "Just as you knew heaven and earth in the beginning without that bringing any variation into your knowing, so you made heaven and earth in the beginning without that meaning a tension between past and future in your activity" ([ca. 400] 1991, 245). Thomas Aquinas also wrestled with the issue of the relationship between eternity and time. Although he and Augustine differ in details, both come to the same fundamental conclusion, namely, there cannot be time "before" creation. Time is a creature and therefore created with creation. God, the primary mover, does not create creation sequentially, step-by-step in a time. Why? Because movement is in time, yet God is eternal. God does not create sequentially in time but in one eternal, creative act. God creates the world *sine motu, ex nihilo* (without motion, out of nothing, Aquinas 1964, 34-39). All of creation is anchored in that beginning, which is not a moment in time but a beginning that has its roots in the Wisdom of God:

> When He established the heavens I was
> there,when He marked out the vaultover the face
> of the deep;When He made firm the skies
> above,When He fixed fast the foundations of the
> earth; When He set for the sea its limit, so that the
> waters should not transgress His command;Then
> was I beside Him as his craftsman.
>
> (Prov. 8:27-29 NAB)

Overtime, Christianity came to understand that this Wisdom, through which creation exists, is the Word of God, the Son of God, Jesus Christ. Saint Paul writes, "He is the first-born of creation, for Him all things were created in heaven and on earth" (Col. 1:15-16). The difference between eternity and time is a dimension of the ontological difference between God and creation. God "is" not the way creation is. It is the nature of the immutable God to exist. Yet it is the nature of nature to have a beginning, to become, to exist through the ever-fleeting moments of time, within the oscillation between being and nothingness (Hegel 1969, 83). For creation, past, present, and future are separated from one another; for the eternal God, they are one. Karl Barth writes,

> God's eternity, like His unity and constancy, is a quality of
> His freedom. It is the sovereignty and majesty of His love in
> so far as this has and is pure duration. The being is eternal in
> whose duration beginning, succession and end are not three
> but one, not separate as first, a second and a third occasion,

but one simultaneous occasion as beginning, middle and end. Eternity is the simultaneity of beginning, middle and end, and to that extent it is pure duration . . . . Time is distinguished from eternity by the fact that in it beginning, middle and end are distinct and even opposed as past, present and future. Eternity is just the duration which is lacking to time, as can be seen clearly at the middle point of time, in the temporal present and in its relationship to the past and the future. Eternity has and is duration which is lacking to time. It has and is simultaneity, temporal present and future. Eternity is just duration. (1957, 608)

It is therefore not possible to extrapolate from created being that is in time to the "being" of God who is eternal. God "is" essentially duration, existence: God is essentially other. Creation is not *in* God but essentially outside of God. Within God, creation would not exist because within God, there is God, not the world! God neither is immanent in the world nor transcends the world: God is essentially other. The relationship between God and creation is not one of immanence or transcendence but of absolute otherness. This is why pantheism and panentheism cannot claim to offer Orthodox Christian perspectives into the mystery of creation.

The absolute otherness of God and creation has to be kept in mind while pondering the relationship between the Christian God and creation. Why? Because the fundamental dogma of Christianity is that God loves creation. Although the love of God surpasses all human understanding, there is an analogy of love between the love of God and the love between human beings. Through this analogy of love, it is possible to see the structure of the relationship between God and creation. As a human being is capable of loving the "otherness" of a beloved person, so does God love creation in ways that surpass all human love. Yet we know by experiencing love that providing the space in which the otherness of the beloved person can become itself is the foundation for any loving relationship. Husband and wife do not live their loving relationship in a model of immanence and transcendence but through the occasionally painful celebration of each other's otherness. Bringing up children is an exercise of how essential it is to provide the space for otherness to become. Letting be as well as respecting and enjoying otherness are fundamental to any loving relationship. It is within this analogy of love that Christians must reflect upon the relationship between God and creation.

Through the life, death, and resurrection of Jesus Christ, God proves his love for the world. Creation came to be through the Word of God, which emptied itself so that creation could be. John writes, "In the beginning was the Word, and the Word was with God and the Word was God. He was in the beginning with God. All things came to be through Him and without Him nothing came to be" (John 1:1-3 NAB). Paul further develops this insight in his first letter to the Colossians (1:15-17 NAB): "He is the image of the invisible God, the firstborn of all creation. For in Him were created all things, in heaven and on earth, the visible and the invisible, whether thrones or dominions or principalities or powers; all things were created through Him and for Him. In Him everything continues in being." Creation, the otherness of God, is created through the Word of God. Creation is not God but created through the Word of God. Hegel understands this to mean that "nature is the Son of God, not as Son however, but as abiding 'otherness'" ([1827] 1970, 206). The philosopher and theologian Vladimir Solovyev unfolds this Hegelian thought in the following way: "God is omnipotent. This is to say that God is not limited. There is no other to God that could limit God. This is because God is otherness within Himself. The otherness of God the Father is God the Son, united with the Father in God the Holy Spirit. This is Hegel's otherness of God within God. The nature of God is Trinitarian" ([1889] 1948, 157-59). Why does God create? Because God the Almighty wants to give existence to nothingness. He wants nothingness, the antithesis of God, to become reality. God wants to give existence to what is outside of God, to give the gift of existence to what is not God. Nothingness has a chance to become something because God's love is so powerful that God is capable of giving his existence away to the otherness outside of God, to nothingness. This insight into the creative act of God has found its expression in the formula *creatio ex nihilo* (creation out of nothing).[2] This gift of existence to creation is a gift truly given. The Word of God, God the Son, the otherness of the Father within God, leaves God, empties itself into nothingness so that creation may be. The gift is the Word of God truly given to the otherness of creation.[3] The Word of God spoken into creation creates the space for creation to become itself, no strings attached. This gift is given to creation so that it can become itself, not God. It is the gift of God's grace, given to creation through his Word, Jesus Christ, that creates creation: "For God so loved the world that He gave His only Son" (John 3:16 NAB). God gave his Son to creation so that creation could become through the Word and for the Word.

Holy Scripture and the Book of Nature

From the Christian perspective, the Word revealed in the Bible and the Word
that creates nature must be the same, because creation springs forth from the
Word of God. The understanding of nature gained by science is therefore
of fundamental importance for a Christian doctrine of creation. Especially
in a time like ours in which so much has been learned, the church must
be fundamentally interested in the worldview gained by science. Without
integrating these insights into its teachings, the church cannot proclaim the
Christian message in a credible way today.[4] What is the most fundamental
discovery made by modern science that a Christian theology of nature
needs to integrate? In my view, it is the discovery that nature is capable of
creating itself. There can no longer be any reasonable doubt that the physical
universe, life, and human beings are the result of the same natural, creative
process. There are so many facts in favor of evolution that it is no longer a
hypothesis or a theory. Evolution is the fundamental law of the universe. A
different question is whether science has discovered how evolution works.
In my opinion, the answer here is yes and no. Yes, because one can argue on
scientific grounds that nature works the same way throughout cosmogenesis.
Evolution consistently brings forth the new through the integration of
the old: atoms from elementary particles, molecules from atoms, life from
integrated molecules. This architecture reflects the creative process by which
nature brings forth novelty: at any dimension, from the smallest patterns
possible to the superstructure of the entire universe, the new emerges from the
integration of what emerged before.[5] New unities emerge through integration
of elements that were previously integrated. This is to say that any new
entity consists of previously integrated entities. At any level, wholes consist
of elements that are wholes themselves yet at a lower level. This hierarchical
architecture is the consequence of the natural creative process. *Higher* and
lower are not value judgments but refer to the historicity by which younger
(higher) hierarchies are dependent upon older (lower) hierarchies. As long as
there is energy left from the original explosion of the big bang, the creative
process will continue bringing forth new hierarchies by integrating older
hierarchies. Even after destructions caused by disasters and catastrophes, the
creative process will start anew. It is creation's nature to continue integrating
the pieces left into new wholes that will serve as basic elements for subsequent
creative steps. The point is that the universal creative process is self-similar
but nonlinear. It is nonlinear because the new has properties that do not exist
at the level of the unintegrated parts. The nature of the creative process is to

create new levels of realities by constantly repeating the two-step process of diversification and integration. As long as there is energy to drive the process, universal morphogenesis does not—and cannot—stop (see Prigogine 1980; Kauffman 1995). Universal Evolution and the Problem of TeleologyIs the process of evolution oriented toward reaching a predetermined goal? Before trying to answer this question, one needs to carefully separate different types of teleological processes. Ernst Mayr does this by distinguishing two types of goal-oriented processes: teleonomic and teleomatic. He writes, "The discovery of the existence of genetic programs has provided a mechanistic explanation of one class of teleological phenomena. A physiological process of a behavior that owes its goal-directedness to the operation of a program can be designated as 'teleonomic'" (1982, 48). Mayr goes on to define teleomatic processes:

> Any process, particularly one relating to inanimate objects in which a definite end is reached strictly as a consequence of physical laws may be designated as "teleomatic." When a falling rock reaches its endpoint, the ground, no goal-seeking or intentional or programmed behavior is involved, but simply conformance to the law of gravitation. So it is with a river inexorably flowing toward the ocean. When a red-hot piece of iron reaches an end state where its temperature and that of its environment are equal, the reaching of this endpoint is, again, due to strict compliance with physical law, the first law of thermodynamics. *The entire process of cosmic evolution, from the first big-bang to the present time, is strictly due to a sequence of teleomatic processes on which stochastic perturbations are superimposed.* (1982, 49; emphasis added)

I fully agree with distinguishing goal-oriented processes that are guided by programs from those that simply follow physical laws. I disagree, however, that evolution is a sequence of teleomatic processes "on which stochastic perturbations are superimposed." I disagree because the falling rock releases energy while the evolutionary process is dependent upon an intake of energy. The falling rock moves toward homogeneity and equilibrium while evolution generates heterogeneity and only occurs in structures far from equilibrium (Prigogine 1980, xi-xix). The result of teleomatic processes is predictable: increasing entropy or degeneration—the result of evolution is decreasing entropy and the unpredictable emergence of new patterns. Teleomatic processes and the process of evolution are essentially different. Cosmogenesis is not a teleomatic process but a process that will generate new patterns. The organization of these patterns, however, is unpredictable because they are the result of what actually happened as opposed to what could also have happened. Evolutionary patterns are essentially probabilistic, historical events with numerous degrees of freedom. One can predict that patterns will form, but how history will shape them is impossible to forecast. I suggest referring to evolutionary pattern formation as teleomorphic processes with the following definition: Teleomorphic processes are oriented toward the generation of increasingly complex patterns the organization of which cannot be predicted. The notion of teleomorphic processes integrates the necessity of emergence with the probabilistic nature of history. Teleomorphic processes, therefore, integrate the predictability that increasingly complex patterns will be generated with the unpredictability of the precise sequence of the historical events that will bring such patterns into reality. Teleomorphic processes combine the predictability of the emergence of increasingly complex patterns with the unpredictability of any essentially probabilistic sequence. Knowing all the parameters of the present does not allow prediction of the future, as S. P. Laplace claimed. The new is not already determined in the past; it emerges as genuine, unpredictable novelty. In my opinion, this summarizes fairly the understanding of evolution by physics and chemistry. Biologists might object because, according to the neo-Darwinistic understanding of evolution, mutation and natural selection is the two-step mechanism that brings forth organismic evolution. I fully agree that natural selection provides the directionality in organismic evolution. However, natural selection can work only on organisms (phenotype), not on their genome (genotype). The fundamental driving force in organismic evolution is toward complexification of genetic programs. Natural selection, through the principle of competition, sorts out what organismic novelty will survive (see n. 8). We start to understand at least some of the mechanisms that led to increasingly complex genotypes. In his book *The Shape of Life*, Rudolf Raff writes, "Evolutionary changes are facilitated by the duplication of genes, including control genes. The duplicated genes are similar to, but distinct from, the ancestral genes, and can be co-opted to carry out related but different functions" (1996, 203). Genes that interact with one another to generate genetic programs can also duplicate. At first, such duplicated programs might simply be redundant; but in a second step, they might become different through mutations. Additional mutations might link a newly generated program with the original one. Such an event might provide the genetic burst necessary for the appearance of significant phylogenetic novelty. Obviously, it might take considerable time for a quantal, evolutionary event to appear in the fossil record. A critical parameter is how fast the new organisms proliferated and spread into environments favorable for their fossilization. This understanding might help explain why evolution is quite frequently punctuated—not gradual.[6] In my view, it is this process of genomic complexification that brings about increasingly complex forms of life. Modern molecular genetics is on the verge of concluding that the driving force of biological evolution is the generation of new genetic programs that control embryonic development. These genetic programs become increasingly complex through duplications of already existing programs, their diversification by mutations, and their integration into new genomes. The process is generating increasing complexity through the pattern of duplication, diversification, and integration. If this is the case, and I think it is, the evolution of organisms would follow the pattern through which complexification is also achieved in physical evolution already at the level of atomic evolution. Complexification in physical as well as in biological evolution would follow the same pattern. This understanding of the evolutionary process suggests that there is an inherent drive toward complexity (not progress!) in nature,[7] a drive to increase complexity by integrating elements into new wholes. The creative process is, however, not teleological but teleomorphic. This is true for the evolution of atoms and molecules as well as for the evolution of life. The important point here is that there is no break in the creative process between physical and organismic evolution. There are lower and higher levels of reality in nature because the creative process integrates elements at one level to construct the next. The reality of each level is dependent upon the structural support of the elements it integrates. Because of the self-similarity of the evolutionary process, unities (or wholes) are hierarchically organized. Integrated parts reach into a level of reality that is not accessible to them in isolation. United, however, the parts are transformed because they become the carriers of a unity that they bring forth through integration. This is similar to a pyramid in that the top reaches into heights that the building blocks cannot reach in isolation. By being integrated into the superstructure of the pyramid, the building blocks participate in the height reached by the top. Each new level, therefore, emerges through unification of previously integrated unities. The highest level of reality that nature has brought forth is human self-consciousness. It emerges from the integration of the conscious and subconscious elements of the human psyche. These emerge from the physiological interactions of the different parts of the human brain. The human mind, conscious of itself in the lucidity of the "I," is the top of a psychic hierarchy that integrates hierarchies of already integrated hierarchies. This, however, is not the structure of only the human mind. The human body is similarly constructed. It consists of integrated organs made of integrated tissues that integrate a diversity of cell types. Each cell is in itself a hierarchy of integrated hierarchies, from its organelles down to chromosomes, DNA, nucleotides, molecules, and atoms. As one disassembles each hierarchy into its parts that are themselves hierarchies, one travels the route of evolution back in time. Cells are younger than the parts they integrate; chromosomes are younger than their genes. These are in turn younger than their molecules, and those are even younger than the atoms from which the molecules were synthesized. Because the universal creative process is self-similar, any entity is a unity of elements that are unities of elements themselves. This is why disintegrating a unity into its elements leads to the discovery that the elements so isolated are integrated unities themselves. This is the imprint left by the self-similarity of the evolutionary process. New complexity emerges from the synthesis of elements that are themselves complex. The discovery of this fundamental architecture of physical as well as biological evolution provides an essential insight: there is no gap between physical and biological evolution.[8] The natural process of general evolution works in the same way at any level. The process does not destroy the previously created elements. It does not melt the elements into some uniform amalgam that is then cast into new forms. Rather, the maintenance of the peculiarity of the elements is a precondition for the synthesis of novelty. There are no tissues without different cell types, no organs without various tissues, and no bodies without a diversity of organs. This hierarchical structure is the consequence of the self-similarity of the natural, creative process of evolution (Brun 1994). The process is creative in that it integrates new hierarchies from hierarchies that, by definition, are integrated entities themselves. The evolutionary process, therefore, is not a random walk but is oriented toward increasing complexity. However, the direction of cosmic evolution toward the generation of hierarchies of integrated hierarchies does not preclude genuine history. The history of the universe is, thus, neither predetermined (teleological) nor random. Evolutionary history integrates the necessity to form patterns with the chance of their historical outcome. The unpredictability is a result of the historical nature of creative events. The probabilistic nature of evolution precludes determinism but includes the chance to increase complexity. Evolution is a creative process that integrates what seems to be mutually exclusive, namely, increasing complexity with undetermined outcome. The nature of the evolutionary process is not teleomatic but teleomorphic. Throughout cosmogenesis, the creative process is consistently the same. This discovery has profound implications for a philosophy of nature.

Does science understand the creativity of nature? Here, I think the answer is a definite no. This is because the methodology of science lends itself to uncovering mechanisms of *how* synthesis brings forth the new. *Why* is it that synthesis creates novelty is not a question in the domain of science. Rather, the question relates to the realm of a metaphysic that is anchored in science but transcends science. The philosopher Karl Popper described this ontological structure of nature precisely: "We live in a universe of emergent novelty" (1974, 281). Such insights are also of fundamental importance for an updated Christian theology of nature because the way nature is creative leads to a deepened understanding of the relationship between nature and human beings. It makes the kinship between human beings and creation explicit. Humans are not placed into this world from the outside but have emerged through the natural creative process from within creation. We are reminded of this fundamental truth by Philip Hefner: "We are, first of all, thoroughly natural creatures. We have emerged from the natural evolutionary processes. These processes have bequeathed to us a constitution that is informed by both genetic and cultural material" (1993, 19). Science brought this blood relationship between human beings and creation into the foreground. For an updated Christian doctrine of creation, the position of human beings in creation needs to be carefully reassessed. Science showed that in spite of human beings living on Earth, Earth is not the center of the universe and human beings are not the goal of evolution. Science puts us into "nowhere" as our place. Why? To better understand the real centrality of our place, which is the kinship between creation and human beings. From the Christian perspective, this place is to faithfully continue the journey of faith: "For creation awaits with eager expectation the revelation of the children of God" (Rom. 8:19 NAB).

UNIVERSAL EVOLUTION AND GOD'S PLAN OF SALVATION

An essential component of the Christian message is that God has a plan for creation: to save it. According to science, cosmogenesis is nothing more than evolutionary history brought about by natural law, not by supernatural guidance. If so, how can God realize his plan to save creation? Does the Christian faith not demand that science demonstrate a plan that guides cosmogenesis toward a predetermined goal? After all, should science not be a servant of theology, supporting theology in its quest for a better understanding of supernatural, eternal truth? Rather than science helping out, however, by demonstrating that nature follows a plan—bringing forth human beings, for example—most scientists cannot find any evidence for such a plot.[9] In my view, the hope of some theologians that one day scientists will discover the Christian history of salvation to be the guiding principle of evolution is a fallacious expectation. The fallacy is reducing dimensions of faith to the dimensions of reality accessible to science. There is no map drawn by science that can guide theologians through the land of faith. Why? Because the history of salvation does not run parallel with the history of creation. The time of faith is not identical to the time of worldly history because salvation is ever-present rather than occurring after history comes to an end. According to the Christian view, the Kingdom of God will not come sometime in the future; it is always already present, has always already arrived.[10] For Christians, some basic questions are: How can God implement his plan to save creation if creation is capable of creating itself? How can God assure the creation of human beings through the natural process if he does not intervene, at least during critical phases in evolution? The critical answer from within Christian theology to both of these questions is that God does not create sequentially in time but *sine motu* (without motion, see the argument by Augustine and Thomas Aquinas cited earlier). Supernatural interventions at critical moments must also be firmly rejected on scientific grounds. After Darwin showed that the interaction between variation and natural selection is sufficient to drive evolution, special creation of human beings could no longer be a reasonable explanation for any phase in organismic evolution (for a detailed rejection of the argument from design, see McMullin 1993). I cannot agree with any interventions of the Creator into the process of cosmogenesis, not for the origin of human beings, the emergence of life, or even during a few milliseconds at the beginning of the universe because such supernatural interventions would jeopardize freedom. If God intervened in the creative process, God would also be responsible for *not* intervening—for accidents, catastrophes, indeed any conceivable evil. If there is manipulation by the Creator at any time during the process of cosmogenesis, then God is to blame for how creation has turned out. In order for the Christian message to make sense, creation needs to be capable of creating itself. This is essential for the loving relationship between God and creation. Creation has to be free to enter into this relationship of love with God. From an Orthodox Christian perspective, God's plan of salvation is executed not by his fine-tuning the big bang or intervening to bring forth life or human beings but through the death and resurrection of Jesus. The question of how it is possible that creation can freely create itself while precisely fulfilling God's plan to save it has to be pondered by keeping in mind the relationship between eternity and time. God is eternal, and so is his saving plan for creation. God does not come up with a plan for creation today and change it tomorrow, for God is eternal, not in time. Eternity and time are essentially different, yet they are united in this difference. The eternal plan of God for creation is precisely executed without negating the genuine history of creation. It is a paradox that eternity and time are united through their difference, not isolated from one another. This paradox cannot be dissolved. It needs to be left standing because it offers a glimpse of what it means to say that God is almighty. The Trinitarian structure of God "being" One in the diversity of three persons is shining through. All of creation—all that exists, including eternity and time—mirrors unity in diversity, the Trinitarian nature of God.

In this view, unity in diversity is the fundamental structure of the relationship between God and creation. At the center of this relationship is the analogy of love, the mutual affirmation and enjoyment of otherness. The love of God for creation is beyond all understanding; our human experience of love, however, allows a glimpse into the central importance of otherness. Without the affirmation and enjoyment of this fundamental structure, there cannot be a loving relationship. Otherness also implies each partner giving the space and freedom to the other for future growth in the loving relationship. Also implicit in the affirmation and enjoyment of otherness is the acceptance of the history through which the beloved partner became what he or she has become. For our understanding, time and eternity exclude one another. Our reason, however, tells us clearly that eternity cannot be limited by time. We understand that eternity and time are essentially different from one another, yet reason sees that they are united in this difference. What does this mean for the problem of how God's plan of salvation relates to cosmic history? It means that cosmic history is not under the tutelage of eternity. Cosmic history can become itself in its domain that consists of past, present, and future. Yet because eternity and time are united through their difference, the eternal plan of God to save creation is real any moment in time. The paradox consists in that creation is free to create itself through its own history; and through this history, the eternal, saving plan of God becomes precisely executed. The paradox is rooted in the essence of love that respects the freedom of the beloved other. How this is possible can be experienced in any loving relationship but is essentially beyond human understanding. There is, however, a historical example that illustrates this paradoxical relationship between eternity and time. It is the passion of Jesus Christ in which the human beings involved were acting freely, executing their own plans; yet by their doing so, the eternal plan of God was precisely executed. I cannot think of a human author capable of writing a play in such a way, an author who lets the actors act whatever they feel is best for them and by doing so precisely execute the play the playwright has envisioned. To my mind, the story of Jesus's life, passion, and resurrection is the most powerful demonstration of the paradox that exists between eternity and time. This paradox of how it is possible that eternity and time are essentially different from one another yet united in this difference is at the heart of the problem. The problem is how the eternal saving plan of God can become reality within the history of time. There is no solution for human understanding, only the paradoxical insight offered by the example of the story of Jesus Christ.

From the view offered through this story, one might see an analogy of how creation can create itself yet precisely fulfill God's plan of salvation. There is, however, no possibility to dissolve this paradox into a solution that can then be analyzed by science. Just as there is no saving plan that can be detected by historical research into the life and death of Jesus Christ, so the history of creation told by science cannot document any plan of a Creator. In both cases, the insight that God has a saving plan for creation is given by faith, not by human or natural history. The fundamental message of Christianity is that God loves His creation. Based on the analogy of love that exists between the love of God and the love of human beings, it becomes obvious, on theological grounds, that creation *has* to create itself. How could it be true that creation is called to be the loving partner of God if creation cannot become itself? How could creation genuinely enter into the loving relationship offered by the Creator if creation cannot refuse it? The freedom of creation to make this choice is fundamental to the Christian message. For without freedom of God *and* creation, the Christian message does not make sense. The discovery made by science that creation is indeed capable of creating itself confirms what is implicit in the fundamental Christian dogma, namely, that God loves creation. It is from this fundamental dogma that any version of supernatural intervention and teleology, including all forms of the anthropic principle, must be rejected.[11]

God and Creation: Faith Seeking Understanding

If the Word of God creates creation and Christian theology holds that it does, then the creative principle that does the creating has to always be the same because the Word of God is eternal—it does not change through time. In my view, science has uncovered this consistency of the natural, creative principle: universal evolution is the result of sequential syntheses. It is the integration of the old that brings forth the new; synthesis is creative. The teleomorphic process that brings forth the entire universe is always the same. This is the first contribution made by science that is essential to a deepened understanding of the Christian faith.

The second contribution that science makes to "faith seeking understanding" is that synthesis never destroys. The elements that synthesis integrates into new wholes do not lose their identity. Rather, they gain a new reality, which creatively transforms them. The elements of a whole gain a new reality because the whole becomes reality through the parts. The elements are *creatively* transformed because the integration of the parts creates a new unity in which the parts participate. This participation of the parts in the whole transforms the parts. They become the carrier of a unity in which by themselves, in isolation, they do not participate. This elevation of the elements into the reality of the whole, their creative transformation, is the hallmark of the entire creative process of cosmogenesis. A third contribution made by science to a better understanding of the Christian faith is ontological in nature. Evolution works by integrating diversity into unity. New existence springs forth from the integration of diversity. The fundamental, ontological structure of all that is demonstrates this fundamental paradox of unity through difference (Heidegger 1960). I see this structure of being as a glimpse of the Word of God in the otherness of nature. God "is" existence as unified diversity of the three divine persons. That anything that is in creation exists as difference in identity mirrors the Trinitarian structure of the nature of God. This nature of God is to "exist" as unity in the diversity of the Father, the Son, and the Holy Spirit. In this view, unified difference brings forth new existence because this ontological structure is the imprint in creation of the Trinitarian nature of God's Word. From the Christian perspective, creation is brought forth by the Word of God that departs from God into the otherness of creation. Through this incarnation into the otherness of creation, the Word of God brings forth creation in time through sequential, creative transformations. What already exists is unified to create the new; parts are integrated to form new wholes. This elevation of the parts into the reality of the whole is the working of the Word of God through its dimension of grace. Grace accepts what already exists and, without destroying these elements, elevates them into a new reality. The incarnated Word of God creatively transforms nothingness into creation step-by-step, letting creation become itself.

From this perspective on creation, one might gain an insight into the sacrament of the Eucharist. Here, too, the elements of bread and wine are not destroyed but are being creatively transformed. In creation, as in the

Eucharist, the Word of God creates not by destroying or replacing what is already there, what already exists, but by elevating the old into the new. For Christians, the celebration of the Eucharist is the culmination of Christian life and worship. In consecration, bread and wine become the body and blood of Jesus Christ. They become a new reality through ontological change (Pope Paul VI [1965] 1981, 172). For Christians, therefore, bread and wine are not just symbols of Christ but *are* Christ. In Thomistic metaphysics, transubstantiation precisely expresses this fundamental belief. It fails, however, to explain why the "accidents" or "species" of bread and wine remain even though the "substances" of bread and wine have become other substances, namely, the body and blood of Christ.

In contrast to the static concept of "eternal substances" in Thomistic metaphysics, we know today that creation is essentially dynamic. Synthesis creates novelty by integrating elements into a higher unity without destroying the peculiarities of the integrated elements. Synthesis creatively transforms the integrated parts into a new whole. This new whole is present in the parts through their particular modes. Integrated parts, therefore, express a reality that in isolation they cannot. Because the whole is real through the integrated parts, the parts become the whole through their peculiarity as elements. This is not (yet) Eucharistic theology but an updated philosophy of nature. It attempts to integrate the most fundamental insights into the nature of the universe obtained by modern science. Eucharistic theology will have to integrate this essentially new understanding of nature because the Word of God in creation and present in the Eucharist is the same. This view suggests that creative transformation is the principle of creation and the Eucharist. The notion of creative transformation is quite close to the old explanation of the Eucharistic mystery by transubstantiation as consubstantiation.[12] Yet the concept of creative transformation might provide a better insight into the mystery of the sacrament. The substance of the body and blood of Christ and the substances of bread and wine are not on the same level of reality but form a hierarchy. In this new hierarchy, bread and wine are creatively transformed into the body and blood of Jesus Christ. Through consecration, bread and wine become integrated into this new reality in such a way that they become this reality without being destroyed. Through this interaction, the elements of bread and wine are not replaced but elevated by the real presence of the Lord. Creative transformation, the principle through which the Word of God creates the new from the old, is the same in the Eucharist and creation. Creative transformation does not replace or dispose of what has been previously created. Rather, throughout cosmogenesis, as well as in the

Eucharist, the old is elevated into the new by the nature of God's grace. The sacrament of the Eucharist is, therefore, not "out of this world." It sheds light on the sacramental character of creation. The mystery of the Eucharist as well as the mystery of creation is impenetrable; they illuminate one another.

Creation is essentially revelation of God because creation is His Word spoken *into* creation. Creation, therefore, is essentially self-manifestation of God in the otherness of creation. At the center of creation is the gift of God of Himself—so that creation can become. This gift from God the Father, namely, his Son, the Word of God, is the gift to creation. It is this gift that enables creation to create itself, namely, the otherness of God. The Word of God departs from God into nothingness so that otherness of God, creation, can become. Creation is therefore not out of God but out of nothing. Yet through this gift of the Word of God to creation, creation participates in the nature of God through its essential otherness. How God and otherness of God can be one is visible in the Word of God incarnate, Jesus Christ. In him and for him is everything that is. "He is the firstborn of creation, for in him all things were created in heaven and on earth" (Col. 1:15-16 NAB).

Creation is the first and fundamental sacrament because creation participates in the nature of God through this essential otherness. Langdon Gilkey expresses the heart of the matter when he writes, "To know God truly is to know God's presence also in power, the life, the order, and the redemptive unity of nature. Correspondingly, to know nature truly is to know its mystery, its depth, and its ultimate value—it is to know nature as an image of the sacred, a visible sign of an invisible grace" (1993, 204). For Christians, this becomes visible reality in the birth of Christ. In Christ, the Word of God, who is God, and the Word of God in the otherness of creation, is demonstrably one. In Christ, creation and God are united *in the difference*—not flat sameness. Through the unification of creation with God in Christ, creation participates in the nature of God. It is this unification of God and creation that makes creation sacred.

The mystery of creation as well as the sacrament of the Eucharist is incomprehensible because both have their origin in the Word of God.

NOTES

1. For a summary of different views and models of how God might relate to creation, see Peters (1996).
2. For a history of what led to this insight, see Gerhard May's *Creatio Ex Nihilo* ([1978] 1994).

3. Jorgen Molt Mann (1985) pursues a similar appreciation.

4. I am quite sure that I'm not alone in appreciating the interest that the current pope has in these important matters. See for example, John Paul II (1990). For the necessity to rethink the Christian faith to make it reasonable again to believe in our time, see Hall (1996).

5. The magazine *Nature* carried an article (Pascrell et al. 1996) that described how galaxies might have formed through the merger of subgalactic clumps (but also see Scodeggio 2001).

6. This view is based on Stuart Kauffman's contributions on the functioning of genetic networks on one hand (Kauffman 1993, 407) and on the model of punctuated equilibria proposed by Niles Eldredge and Stephen Jay Gould (1972) on the other.

7. Already, G. W. Leibniz and J. B. Lamarck suggested such a drive in nature. I think they were both right. The problem, however, was that Lamarck equated complexity and progress. The notion of progress depends on value judgments, complexity does not. The level of complexity could perhaps be quantified by determining how many hierarchies the hierarchy of interest integrates.

8. Among biologists, the notion that organismic evolution is essentially different from physical evolution is still widespread. Biologists argue that evolution works through the two-step process of mutations and natural selection. Because there is no individual variation between atoms or molecules of the same kind, natural selection cannot select. Therefore, some biologists argue, one should not use the concept of evolution for the "so-called evolution in different areas" (Mayr 1982, 627). From my perspective, biologists who argue in this way miss an important point. It is that organismic evolution, at least at the level of phyletic evolution, depends on complexification of the genome. We start to understand some of the mechanisms that bring forth increasing genomic complexity. Natural selection works postfactum on the new phenotype brought forth by genomic complexification. The point is that complexification is at the base of both, physical as well as organismic evolution.

9. In recent years, some physicists have advocated that there is a principle at work in nature to bring forth human beings (see Barrow and Tipler 1988). There are different understandings and definitions of this anthropic principle. Errol E. Harris thinks that such a principle is philosophically justified. See Harris (1991); Russell, Murphy, and Isham (1993).

10. I'm greatly indebted to Pierre Teilhard de Chardin's work. I do not believe, however, that the history of evolution, including human history, is oriented toward a predetermined goal (Ω) because such determinism would preclude human freedom. Without freedom, there could be no loving relationship between God and creation.

11. I therefore have to disagree with Joseph M. Życiński (1996) that the weak anthropic principle gives credence to an argument from design.

12. For a discussion of the term *consubstantiation* and its origin, see Plotnik (1970, 32-33).

REFERENCES

Aquinas, Thomas. [ca. 1270] 1964. *Summa Theologiae.* Ia, 45.3; 45.4. New York: McGraw-Hill, Blackfriars Press.

Augustine. [ca. 400] 1972. *The City of God.* Trans. Henry Bettenson. Harmondsworth, Middlesex, England: Penguin.

————. [ca. 400] 1991. *Confessions.* Trans. Henry Chadwick. Oxford: Oxford Univ. Press.

Barth, Karl. 1957. *Church Dogmatics. The Doctrine of God.* II/2. New York: Charles Scribner's Sons.

Barrow, J. D., and F. J. Tipler. 1988. *The Anthropic Cosmological Principle.* Oxford: Oxford Univ. Press.

Brun, Rudolph B. 1994. "Integrating Evolution: A Contribution to the Christian Doctrine of Creation." *Zygon: Journal of Religion and Science* 29 (September): 275-96.

Eldredge, Niles, and Stephen Jay Gould. 1972. "Punctuated Equilibria: An Alternative to Phyletic Gradualism." In *Models in Palaeobiology,* ed. T. Schopf, 119-30. San Francisco: Freeman, Cooper and Co.

Gilkey, Langdon. 1993. *Nature, Reality and the Sacred: The Nexus of Science and Religion.* Minneapolis: Augsburg Fortress.

Hall, Douglas John. 1996. "The Future of Protestantism in North America." *Theology Today* 52: 458-65.

Harris, E. E. 1991. *Cosmos and Anthropos: A Philosophical Interpretation of the Anthropic Cosmological Principle.* New Jersey and London: Humanities Press International.

Hefner, Philip. 1993. *The Human Factor: Evolution, Culture, and Religion.* Minneapolis: Fortress Press.

Hegel, G. W. F. [1827] 1970. *Philosophy of Nature*. Ed. and trans. M. J. Perry. London: Allen and Unwin, and New York: Humanities Press.

————. 1969. *Logic. G. Hegel's Science of Logic*. Trans. A. V. Miller. London: George Allen and Unwin, and New York: Humanities Press.

Heidegger, M. 1960. *Essays in Metaphysics: Identity and Difference*. Trans. Kurt. F. Leidecker. New York: Philosophical Library.

John Paul II. 1990. *On Science and Religion; Reflections on the New View from Rome*. Ed. R. J. Russell, W. R. Stoeger, S. J., and G. V. Coyne. Vatican City State: Vatican Observatory Publications, distributed by The Univ. of Notre Dame Press.

Kauffman, Stuart A. 1993. *The Origins of Order, Self-Organization and Selection in Evolution*. New York: Oxford Univ. Press.

————. 1995. *At Home in the Universe*. New York: Oxford Univ. Press.

May, Gerhard. [1978] 1994. *Creatio Ex Nihilo*. Trans. A. S. Worrall. Edinburgh: T. & T. Clark.

Mayr, Ernst. 1982. *The Growth of Biological Thought: Diversity, Evolution, and Inheritance*. Cambridge: Harvard Univ. Press, Belknap Press.

McMullin, Ernan. 1993. "Evolution and Special Creation." *Zygon: Journal of Religion and Science* 28 (September): 299-335.

Moltmann, Jürgen. 1985. *God in Creation: A New Theology of Creation and the Spirit of God*. The Gifford Lectures 1984-1985. San Francisco: Harper and Row.

Pascarelle, S. M., R. A. Windhorst, W. C. Keel, and S. C. Odewahn. 1996. "Sub-galactic Clumps at a Redshift of 2.39 and Implications for Galaxy Formation." *Nature* 383 (5 September): 45.

Paul VI. [1965] 1981. "Mysterium fidei." Encyclical. In *The Papal Encyclicals 1958-1981*. Raleigh, N.J.: McGrath.

Peters, Ted. 1996. "Theology and Science: Where Are We?" *Zygon: Journal of Religion and Science* 31 (June): 323-43.

Plotnick, Kenneth. 1970. *Hervaus Natalis OP and the Controversies of the Real Presence and Transubstantiation*. München: Ferdinand Schöningen.

Popper, Karl. 1974. *Unended Quest: An Intellectual Autobiography*. LaSalle, Ill.: Open Court.

Prigogine, Ilya. 1980. *From Being to Becoming: Time and Complexity in the Physical Sciences*. San Francisco: Freeman.

Raff, Rudolph A. 1996. *The Shape of Life: Genes, Development, and the Evolution of Animal Form*. Chicago: Univ. of Chicago Press.

Russell, Robert J., Nancey Murphy, and C. J. Isham, eds. 1993. *Quantum Cosmology and the Laws of Nature: Scientific Perspectives on Divine Action*.

Vatican City State: Vatican Observatory Publications, and Berkeley, Calif.: The Center for Theology and the Natural Sciences.

Scodeggio, Marco. 2001. "Toward Resolving the Mystery of Galaxy Formation." *Science* 294 (19 October): 537-38.

Solovyev, Vladimir. [1889] 1948. *Russia and the Universal Church*. London: G. Bless.

Życiński, Joseph M. 1996. "The Weak Anthropic Principle and the Design Argument." *Zygon: Journal of Religion and Science* 31 (March): 115-30.

STRICT NATURALISM AND CHRISTIANITY: ATTEMPT AT DRAFTING AN UPDATED THEOLOGY OF NATURE

(*Zygon*, vol. 42, no. 3 [September 2007])

Abstract.   The first part of this paper sketches a view on cosmogenesis from the perspective of modern science. The emphasis is on two points. First, the laws of nature are outcomes of the history of nature; they were not imposed on nature from outside of nature. The second point is that the universe (including us human beings) is the result of a single natural process. It consistently brings forth novelty through a probabilistic sequence of syntheses. As a consequence, the new emerges from the unification of elements that were previously unified. This universal creative process is probabilistic and nonlinear. The process is probabilistic (historical) because each creative event occurs within a cohort of also possible events. The creative process is also nonlinear because the new has qualities that its elements (in isolation) do not possess. I'll refer to this model of understanding cosmogenesis as *strict naturalism*. In the second part, I'll argue that deistic and theistic models of cosmogenesis cannot cope with strict naturalism. This is because it excludes teleology and supernatural interference(s) into the creative process. In contrast to deism and theism, I'll try to show that Christianity is capable of integrating strict naturalism. To do that the suggestion is to focus on the Christian notion of incarnation. At the center of this reflection will be the attempt to increase the understanding of Christian faith that only the Word of God creates.

Cosmogenesis: A View from Science

Over the last decade or so, astronomers and physicists have made tremendous progress in better understanding the origin of our universe. They found ways to confirm that the universe emerged from an original explosion. They obtained an amazingly detailed map of what happened. The map shows the distribution of the first patterns of energy and matter. These primary structures of the universe emerged within a fraction of a second of the original explosion of the big bang (Seife 2003, 2038). At that time, some of the forces of nature also came into existence. Scientists do not have the data to understand how this happened. They know from experiments performed in particle accelerators that the forces of nature are carried by particles (Cho 2006, 1302). Some of these formed as the quark-gluon plasma expanded at close to the speed of light. The speculation so far is that at the earliest moment of time, there may have been just one primary force, perhaps quantum gravity, and that the other forces of nature emerged from this original force. It may have split into X particles about 10^{-35} seconds "later." X particles might have carried the (so far also hypothetical) grand unified force, the "electronuclear force." About 10^{-3} seconds later, it split into the electroweak force. This force united electromagnetism with the forces that hold atomic nuclei together and also control some forms of radioactive decay. About 400,000 years after the original explosion, the universe became transparent to light. At this time, four forces had emerged in the universe: gravity, the weak and the strong forces (the two forces that operate at the nuclear level), and the photons that carry electromagnetism (Glanz 1998, 2156). The hypothesis that all forces of nature originated from a single one is supported by the discovery of Z particles in 1982 at the cyclotron of CERN at Geneva, Switzerland. Protons were accelerated one way around the cyclotron. As they traveled close to the speed of light, they were made to collide with antiprotons (antimatter) that sped the opposite way. The crash produced an explosion with temperatures that had existed only within seconds after the big bang. At this temperature, Z particles were detected. The fascinating finding is that Z particles unite two of the fundamental forces of nature, the electromagnetic force and the weak force, into one—the "electroweak force." The discovery that separate forces of nature can reunite is the basis for the hypothesis that at even higher temperatures the electroweak force might merge with the strong nuclear force, the force that holds atomic nuclei together. There is hope that those particles will be detected that mediate this so-far hypothetical electronuclear force. Machines are under construction that may be able to generate the temperatures in which these X particles could show up. If they did, it would be only the second time since the original explosion out of which our universe emerged.

From the discovery of Z particles at CERN and extrapolating from the so-far hypothetical X particles, the assumption is that at the instant of the big bang, only one force, only one natural law, existed. The four basic laws of nature—gravity, the electromagnetic force, the weak and strong forces—came into existence sequentially. The conclusion is that the laws of nature emerged from events in the history of nature and were not imposed on it by some supernatural agent.

From this point of view, the possibility exists that the sequence of events that brought forth the natural laws in our universe could have been different in other universes. Current string theory suggests that there might be myriad universes (Witten 2005, 1085).

If so, we are just lucky that in ours, the laws of nature are such that life, including humans, could evolve (Brumfiel 2006, 10). I like the idea of multiverses because it avoids the belief that some supernatural agency fine-tuned the parameters of cosmogenesis so that life and human beings could evolve. Nature is deeply probabilistic, and it seems to me unlikely that the explosion from which our universe originated stands alone. Rather, this "original" event likely happened zillions of times, and our universe emerged from within a cohort of multiverses in which the laws of nature are very different. From this point of view, the laws in our universe emerged from chance events and were not designed or fine-tuned by a supernatural power so that life, including human beings, could evolve.

Some History of Matter.   We are far from a complete understanding of what happened during the birth of our universe. We do know that it emerged sequentially from an original explosion. Although the universe has been cooling from this tremendous event of the big bang for some 13.7 billion years, scientists have measured the afterglow of the explosion. They have found that there still is a pattern generated by those areas that were slightly cooler than others, a patchwork of spots left by the uneven distribution of radiation energy. The first matter-antimatter elementary particles condensed out of the radiation field within a time shorter than the blink of an eye. Most of the energy of the big bang froze into dark matter, matter we cannot see. Only about 5 percent crystallized into matter that lit up, some of which became organized into galaxies and stars. Astronomers have quite recently discovered that there is also dark energy, a force that continues to increase the speed of the expansion of the universe (Brumfiel 2003, 108).

The first stars emerged from collapsing clouds of primary gases, hydrogen and helium. When some areas in these clouds contain slightly more matter than other regions by chance, the heavier areas attract matter from their surroundings. These at first only slightly denser regions grow by attracting increasing amounts of nearby matter. The gravitational collapse compresses the converging gaseous matter, heating it to temperatures high enough to fuse hydrogen into helium, which in turn produces so much heat that the collapsing gas ignites. A nuclear furnace forms in which hydrogen burns and, in the process, fuses into helium. Helium atoms, however, are slightly lighter than the four hydrogen nuclei that fused to form it in the nuclear reaction. The missing matter is transformed into energy according to Einstein's famous formula $E=mc^2$. This energy generated at the center of the forming star counteracts the gravitational collapse. Equilibrium is established between the gravitational force, tending to make the star collapse into itself and the heat generated by nuclear forces, an equilibrium that is stable until the fuel at the center of the star is used up. If this happens, gravity wins, and the star begins to collapse. The matter at the core is heated further by pressure of the gravitational force until temperatures are reached at which the carbon atoms fuse with remaining neutrons to form more massive atoms. The accretion of its matter causes friction. The center of the collapsing star heats up again until temperatures are reached at which the helium atoms fuse. The energy generated by this reaction counterbalances the gravitational force again until the nuclear fuel is running out. New generations of stars form in which heavier and heavier atoms emerge, thanks to nuclear fusion processes. The process stops abruptly with the fusion of iron, and a catastrophic implosion ensues. It results in a supernova explosion in which the remaining elements such as nickel, cobalt, gold, and silver are synthesized.

The point is that all naturally occurring elements listed in the Periodic Table of the Elements emerged overtime. They are sequentially synthesized in the nuclear furnaces of the stars. As they age and run out of fuel, the heaviest atoms form during the explosions in supernova events. The chart, therefore, summarizes a part of the physical history of the universe. Moving from the left side of this table to the right traces successive events in the evolution of matter. These events produced the increasing complexity of the heavier elements from the simplest possible organization of subatomic particles in hydrogen atoms. Already in the physical universe, there was complexification. There still is.

Probabilistic Complexification, or How Nature Creates. What can we say about how nature builds increasing complexity? I think the answer is through historical sequences of synthetic events. The pathways of sequential syntheses are not predetermined or goal oriented but rather historical. By historical, I mean that cosmogenesis proceeds through probabilistic events.

This is, each event opens a landscape of future possible creative steps. The emerging statistical landscapes contain the probabilistic cohorts of possible trajectories. The directions the processes may take are within this landscape. Exactly which pathway a process will actually pursue, however, is open because the time of the future is different from the time of the past; the future is open, but the past is closed.

The results of probabilistic complexification do not just pile up hodgepodge. Rather, the process brings forth complexity in which the elements are integrated. True complexity emerges from the unification of parts into wholes, or unities. Their parts unite in such a way that their individual properties still exist, but the unification of their qualities brings forth new properties of the whole. This new reality of the whole transcends the parts because the whole has qualities that the individual parts do not have (Ehrenfels [1891] 1985, 85). Unification brings forth novelty.

Synthesis, the unification of difference into unity, is creative. As I see it, the unification of diversity into unity is the universal creative principle. It is therefore also the creative principle of the evolutionary processes on Earth.

Earth and all of the other planets formed roughly 4.5 billion years ago. Our solar system emerged from a molecular cloud that formed from elements ejected from a supernova explosion. Over about one billion years, the young and fiery Earth cooled to temperatures at which life could exist (Rasmussen et al. 2004, 963). How life began, we do not know. Most likely, molecules aboard comets and meteors that crashed into the forming planet seeded the complex chemistry that led to prelife molecules. We do know that it took only about 500 million years for living things to appear after Earth had cooled for 1.5 billion years. Considering that the universe is 13.7 billion years old, 500 million years is quite short. This suggests that the emergence of life must be a relatively easy process, which provides the basis for the hypothesis that life also formed elsewhere in the universe.

Once life appeared on Earth, competition for life's resources began. To multiply is the primary task of all organisms; only through replication can life continue through the flow of time. Not all of the information necessary to reconstruct life for the next generation is equally well suited for the task. At any given time, there is variation between the individuals of a group of organisms. Some are slightly more efficient than others at reproducing in the existing environment. As a consequence, they outcompete the other individuals in the group. This is the Darwinian law of variation (by chance) and natural selection. Organisms adapt to an ever-changing environment in the creative two-step process of variation and natural selection. Survival of the fittest is the law of life that emerges together with the emergence of life. It must be added to the list of the emerging laws of nature previously mentioned. The law of natural selection is a powerful example that the laws of nature emerge within the history of nature; they are not imposed from outside of nature.

The Complexification of Organisms. As far as we can tell, the human brain is the most complex structure that nature has yet produced. How it works to bring forth self-consciousness is a matter of current research. There are, however, significant clues in anatomy of how nature put our brain together. One way to trace its evolutionary history is to dissect it into its anatomical components. This method leads to the result that parts of our brain came together when reptiles and amphibians evolved. Some components date back even further, to the time fish first appeared roughly 400 million years ago. By dissecting the human brain into its parts, we isolate older and older components. If we continue the process in our mind's eye, these components come together by even more ancient elements: cells. And if we dissect cells into their organelles, we find that these cellular components are older still; some of them, like bacteria, were once free-living organisms. If we keep dissecting, we find that the genetic material in these ancient organisms is composed of unities that are older still. The molecules that make up the genetic information are composed of atoms. As I have pointed out, atoms, including those that make up the chemical components of life, were synthesized in the stars. Any form of life, from the first replicating molecules to cells to multicellular organisms, emerged from a sequence of synthetic events. Once nature brings forth the working structures of life, it usually does not change them significantly. For example, cells have been around for about a billion years, yet their fundamental organization has not changed. Nature rather builds new things by repetitive arrangements of structures that already work, of modules already available. Cells are the modules from which multicellular organisms emerged. They evolved from colonies of cells that first were all the same. Then the division of labor between the cellular modules increased the efficiency of propagation. Some cells were sorted out for reproduction while others became specialized in gathering nutrients. The increased efficiency in extracting energy from the environment made it possible for organisms to become larger. As a consequence, the number of cells and cell types increased (Bonner 1988, 220). Division of function among the various cell types and their proliferation brought forth the various organs. As the environment changed, organisms had to change with it. Those forms of life that could even slightly better cope with the new circumstances increased in numbers while others decreased or disappeared. This is Darwinism: new species emerging from the natural two-step process of variation (between the individuals of a species) and natural selection. For decades, biologists have accumulated data, showing that this mechanism is working. For example, cells frequently form in tissue cultures that have properties significantly different from those of the cells from which they originated. There are also statistically significant (and beautifully performed) field experiments, the results of which clearly demonstrate that variation and natural/sexual selection are powerful mechanisms of evolutionary change. They work not only in laboratories but also in nature (see Ridley 1992, 328). These experiments leave no doubt that Darwin was correct. In his time, however, there was no knowledge of how variations originated. The science of genetics started to flourish about half a century later; and it provided the insight that genes could spontaneously change and, in this way, alter the appearance of organisms. Variation was the result of mutating genes. This insight led to neo-Darwinism, the view that mutations and natural selection drive the evolution of organisms.

Today, molecular geneticists have gained exciting new insights into the nature of mutations. Nucleotides, the modules that constitute DNA, may change and, in this way, produce new organismic traits. However, the genes that an organism possesses are organized into an overarching physiological whole: the genome. It is hierarchically organized, meaning that not all genes are equal. There are regulatory genes—super genes that control entire batteries of subordinate genes. As an embryo develops, regulatory genes are activated first. They activate secondary regulatory genes that turn on the appropriate genetic information necessary to construct the body of the embryo. The formation of a new adult from a fertilized egg is dependent upon a complicated genetic program.

We know that such programs already existed in Vendian/Cambrian times, 500-600 million years ago, thanks to the discovery of amazingly well-preserved fossils of early embryonic stages (Bengston and Zhao 1997, 1645). In addition, we know from fossils discovered in the Canadian Rockies that there was an amazing variety of soft-body organisms (Briggs, Erwin, and Frederick 1994, 217). Skeletal elements did show up rather suddenly about 530 million years ago (Raff 1996, 89). There were sponges; worms; mollusks; echinoderms (sea urchins, for example); trilobites and many types of creatures that died out. Surprisingly, the architecture—whether to be an insect, an arthropod, or a vertebrate—emerged perhaps as far back as 800 million years ago (Runnegar 1994, 369). If so, the genetic programs necessary for the development of these different basic body types had already been assembled. The genes that provided the components of these developmental programs must have come from the already existing unicellular organisms. How they were brought together, we do not know. The genes may have been transferred by viruses. There is an enormous reservoir of genes in the myriad viruses in seawater (Hamilton 2006, 683). Perhaps viruses transported genes between cells that led to the assembly of the first multicellular genomes.

We do know that once a program became assembled for the construction of a specific body type (a phylum), it did not change anymore. Consequently, the "thirty-five living phyla probably all had their origins in the Cambrian, many of them in the Burgess Shale" (Raff 1996, 95). Molecular analysis confirms this stability. Those parts of the developmental programs that organize the different body plans have not changed over hundreds of millions of years. There is a fundamental component in the developmental programs that does not vary. Evolution cannot change this part of a genetic network because it provides the basic regulatory architecture for the construction of a specific body type (Davidson and Douglas 2006, 796). Because of this fundamental principle of construction, any change in this part of the program is lethal. The genetic information involved in the differentiation of organisms within phyla into classes, orders, families, and species came later. The genes necessary for this differentiation emerged through duplications and variations (by mutation) of already existing genetic components.

Over the last decade or so, advances in molecular genetics have advanced tremendously. The main finding is that gene regulation is a multidimensional and extremely complex matter (Zamore and Benjamin 2005, 1519).

Darwin was correct that evolution works by variation and natural selection. Variation, however, is the result of processes that not only alter genomes by mutations but also change how genes are regulated. If genes were the keys on a keyboard, regulation would be the order in which they were played. One can play many tunes not by inventing new keys but by changing the order. To find out how nature accomplished the complexification of organisms from bacteria to human beings remains a project under construction. This, however, does not imply that the process of complexification is somehow beyond the capabilities of nature.

Models of UnderstandingThis may be a good time to lay my cards on the table. I have a fundamental disagreement with deism, the belief that God fine-tuned creation to reach a predetermined goal. I can understand the history of this claim. As scientists discovered that the world was not created more or less at once but came into existence through a historical sequence, the outcome of this sequence had to be somehow determined. How could God's plan for creation be realized if God was not controlling the process? One suggestion was to understand creation as clockwork: God made the clock and wound it up, and creation was ticking along a determined mechanical path. Natural laws, ordained by God, made certain that the pathway of creation could not deviate from the goal set in the beginning.

Darwin showed that this deistic view of creation did not fit the history of life. As science progressed in understanding that biological evolution is not determined but is the outcome of probabilistic historical events, the deistic-mechanical understanding of cosmogenesis became untenable.

In the first part of the twentieth century, it became increasingly obvious that not only life but also the physical universe evolved. Physicists and astronomers worked out in ever-greater detail how what we call matter emerged through a historical sequence of events. Some theologians took notice of this new way of understanding how the world came into existence. The challenge for them was, and still is, how God's purpose for creation could be fulfilled through a historical, not predetermined, process. Process thinkers suggest various ways of how God may be involved in guiding cosmogenesis (Russell et al. 1993, 1). Some argue that God's creativity is constituting, supporting, and proliferating the capacities of creation (Gregersen 1999, 118). How does God do that? "God is seen as reshaping the possibilities as the history goes along, by acting in different ways in different contexts" (Gregersen 1998, 359). Scientists would never notice these supernatural interventions because they are camouflaged within the uncertainty of outcomes in the history of nature. Supernature would be involved either all the time or at those times when the outcome really counts. God's stealth interventions into the history of nature—for example, at the quantum level—would make it impossible in principle for scientists to understand how nature really works. My problem with this kind of thinking is that it makes the work of scientists a joke. It undermines their search for truth even at the level open to scientific investigations. This view favors the position that what science finds out about nature cannot be relevant to theology. Why? Because the reality that science investigates is a dimension not of nature but of supernature. For example, "God is the creator of the fixed laws of elementary particle physics (a nonnegotiable position)" (Gregersen 1998, 364, n 21.1). If this is so, what is left for particle physicists to find out? I have a fundamental disagreement with philosophers and theologians who suggest that the complexity of nature results from supernatural intervention. Not in the beginning, not on its way, and not in the "end" (if there is one) is cosmogenesis guided by aiming, intervening, or goal setting. I am not a theist, but I do appreciate the efforts made by process thinkers. They clearly see the mystery that shrouds the creativity of nature. My disagreement with theistic thought is that it strips this mystery from nature and places it into supernature. By doing so, the mystery of nature becomes an abstraction instead of being concrete in all that nature brings into existence. Furthermore, claiming that nature transcends into supernature cripples nature. It denies nature the power of really and fully becoming itself. Cosmogenesis becomes more or less a function of supernatural tutelage.

I am bonded to my colleagues in science. The ones I know believe that cosmogenesis is the exclusive outcome of an entirely natural process. I share their conviction of strict naturalism. That Christianity should integrate this view from science will hopefully become more intelligible in what follows. If Christianity wants to be in harmony with the discoveries of modern science, and I think it must, an updated Christian theology of nature has to integrate strict naturalism.

How can this be done? There are biblical signs that indicate the path toward this goal. The first mark, in the first chapter of Genesis, identifies the trailhead clearly. The text is unambiguous: God speaks and creation becomes. The trailhead is clearly marked. It is a rock that bears the bold inscription "The Word of God creates!" From here, one can make out a second pointer that indicates the direction in which to go. On it is a sign that reads, "For just as rain and snow fall from heaven and do not return there without saturating the earth and making it germinate and sprout, and providing seed to sow and food to eat, so my Word that comes from my mouth will not return to me empty, but it will accomplish what I please, and will prosper in what I send it [to do]" (Isa. 55:10-11 NAB).

From here, we pursue the task, attempting to construct a way toward an updated Christian understanding of cosmogenesis. An unexpected sharp turn leads to the next marker. We are baffled by the following revelation on it: "In the beginning was the Word, and the Word was with God, and the Word was God . . . . All things came to be through him, and without him nothing came to be" (John 1:1, 3 NAB). The first part of the text, "In the beginning was the Word," is familiar. It reaffirms what we were already told by the message on the trailhead: that the Word of God is the origin of all beginning, of all that is, of all creation. The second part, however, that "the Word was with God and the Word was God," is surprising. It lets us know that God is not alone, that God is with his Word that is God also. If the Word of God is also God and Christianity believes that it is, this Word of God is the perfect expression of God. If it were not, it would not be God. God's word, therefore, is God but the perfect expression of God. Therefore, the Word of God is not identical with God but is rather God's perfect expression. It is God the Son: "God from God, Light from Light, begotten not made, one in Being with the Father" (Nicene Creed [Schaff (1910) 1919, 24]). There is "otherness held in love" *within* God, as G. W. F. Hegel puts it ([1827] 1970, 206).

This, however, is not all that this text reveals. The second sentence is again clear and straightforward: through the Word of God, through the Son of God, "all things came to be through him, and without him nothing came to be." "Through him all things were made" (Creed). There is otherness not only within God but also outside of God. "God has two revelations, as nature and as spirit, and both manifestations are temples which He fills, and in which He is present. God as an abstraction is not true God; His truth is the positing of his other, the living process, the world which is his Son when it is comprehended in its divine form" (Hegel [1827] 1970, 204). This sheds light into the depth of what was previously revealed, namely, that the "Word that comes from my mouth will not return to me empty, but it will accomplish what I please, and will prosper in what I send it [to do]." The text clarifies that this departure of the Word of God that is God into that which is not God is an essential transformation, not just an increase in distance. God who is absolute eternal existence departs from God to bring forth created existence, existence that must become in time. The Word of God that is God becomes that which is not God. God the Son, the otherness of God within God, departs into nothingness, the otherness of God outside of God. "For from him and through him and for him are all things" (Rom. 11:36 NAB). "For in him were created all things" (Col. 1:16 NAB). "[God] spoke to us through a son . . . through whom he created all things" (Heb. 1:2 NAB). "[Jesus Christ] through whom all things are and through whom we exist" (1 Cor. 8:6 NAB).

Christianity insists that the Word of God that is God brings forth that which is not God but creation. This is neither pantheism nor panentheism; the Word of God that is God does not cease to "exist." Creation is not God, as I understand pantheism to suggest, but rather essentially "otherness" of God. I cannot see how the various models of panentheism help in constructing a Christian theology of nature. The Christian revelation about creation does not proclaim that creation is an extension or a function embedded in God. Rather, the Word of God that *is and remains God* is given away to creation. It is a gift that empowers creation to become itself. How can it be that the Word of God remains God yet also becomes the creative center of creation is beyond human understanding. It is a paradox of Christian faith that human logic cannot resolve. There is a light, however, that illuminates this paradox from another incomprehensible event: the mystery of Christmas. In this event, true God becomes truly human. God becomes that which God is not, a human being. As I see it, the mystery of Christmas illuminates the mystery of creation. Christmas is the demonstration that God can be God in that which is not God.

The attempt to construct a trail toward an updated understanding of creation has led us from Genesis to Christmas. From here, a view opens into the mystery that cloaks creation. From the mystery of incarnation shines a light in which one can see that Christmas and creation belong together. They belong together because the Word of God becomes otherness of God in creation and in the Christmas event. Pope John Paul II, addressing the bishops of the Catholic Church in a letter, wrote, "The mystery of the Incarnation will always remain the central point of reference for an understanding of the enigma of human existence, the created world and God himself. The challenge of this mystery pushes philosophy to its limits, as reason is summoned to make its own a logic which brings down the walls within which it risks being confined" (1998, 84).

God's logic of incarnation, the paradox that God can be God in that which is not God, is the foundation of creation. The Word of God incarnate in creation is that creative center from which all creativity of nature originates. This creative center is the Word of God that is God but departs from God is given away to creation so that creation may become. The philosophical question "what is the nature of Nature?" finds here its answer: the nature of Nature is the Word of God given away to creation. It is thanks to this creative gift that creation is capable of becoming itself.

If nature is free to become itself, how will God's plan for creation become reality? Our freedom of action is not an obstacle in Almighty God's plan becoming concrete. Consider Good Friday. All actors in this drama act freely, and yet precisely through their decisions made freely, the saving plan of God becomes executed with absolute precision. Even the cock crows at the right time, and exactly twice!

How then may we outline a Christian understanding of cosmos and creation? I think that such a sketch will show that creation is thanks to the creative Word of God. It will further help to understand that this Word that is God is given away to that which is not God. It is through this gift truly given away, no strings attached, that nothing could become something. In this view, cosmogenesis results from the creative source of nature. This source is the Word of God incarnate in creation. How is it possible to integrate strict naturalism into Christianity? Perhaps by anchoring the model of cosmogenesis constructed by science in God's logic of incarnation. That God is love is the fundamental revelation of Christianity. I therefore trust that creation is the gift of the loving God. This gift is God's creative Word. It becomes the creative center of nature. It empowers nature to freely become itself. Thanks to this freedom, nature is capable of bringing forth creatures that are free. We are these creatures that evolved from within the natural process. As a consequence, human beings belong to nature—we are *"At Home in the Universe"* (Kauffman 1995).

Christianity goes one step further and proclaims that human beings are not only rooted in creation but are the representatives of creation: "Creation awaits with eager expectation the revelation of the children of God" (Rom. 8:19 NAB). We are those free creatures, capable of either accepting or rejecting the loving relationship offered by the Creator.

Conclusion

In the view from science on cosmogenesis that I have sketched, strict naturalism is essential. I have argued that it is also essential to Christianity because the freedom of nature to become itself is the condition for free creatures to emerge. Human beings are these creatures, free to either accept or reject the loving relationship offered by the Creator. Strict naturalism, therefore, only makes explicit what is already implied in the fundamental revelation of Christianity, namely, that God is love.

Note: A version of this article was presented at the XXV Annual Cosmos and Creation Conference at Loyola College, Baltimore, Maryland, June 9-11, 2006.

I thank Professor William R. Graham, TCU Department of Physics; Professor C. David Grant, TCU Department of Religion; and Professor James A. Rurak, Boston College, for the critical reading and comments on early drafts.

References

Bengston, Stefan, and Yue Zhao. 1997. "Fossilized Metazoan Embryos from the Earliest Cambrian." *Science* 277: 1645-48.

Bonner, John. 1988. *"The Evolution of Complexity by Means of Natural Selection.* Princeton: Princeton Univ. Press.

Briggs, Derek, Douglas Erwin, and Frederick Collier. 1994. *The Fossils of the Burgess Shale*. Washington and London: Smithsonian Institution.

Brumfiel, Geoff. 2003. "Cosmology Gets Real." *Nature* 422: 108-10.

_____. 2006. "Outrageous Fortune." *Nature* 439: 10-11.

Cho, Adrian. 2006. "High Energy Physics: Aging Atom Smasher Runs All Out in Race for Most Coveted Particle." *Science* 312: 1302-03.

Davidson, Erich, and Douglas Erwin. 2006. "Gene Regulatory Networks and the Evolution of Animal Body Plans." *Science* 311: 796-800.

Ehrenfels, Christian von. [1891] 1985. "On Gestalt Theory." Revised and expanded English version of "Mach und Ehrenfels: Über Gestaltqualitäten und das Problem der Abhängigkeit," in *Christian von Ehrenfels: Leben und Werk*, ed. R. Fabian, 85-111. Amsterdam: Rodopi.

Glanz, James. 1998. "Cosmic Motion Revealed." *Science* 282: 2156- 57.

Gregersen, Niels Henrik. 1998. "The Idea of Creation and the Theory of Autopoietic Processes." *Zygon: Journal of Religion and Science* 33: 333-67.

_____. 1999. "Autopoiesis: Less than Self-constitution, More than Self-organization. Reply to Gilkey, McClelland and Deltete, and Brun." *Zygon: Journal of Religion and Science* 34: 117-38.

Hamilton, Garry. 2006. "The Gene Weavers." *Nature* 441: 683-85.

Hegel, G. W. F. [1872] 1970. *Philosophy of Nature*. Ed. and trans. M. J. Petry. London: Humanities.

John Paul II. 1998. "Fides et Ratio." Encyclical Letter to the Catholic Bishops of the Church (September). Vatican City: Holy See.

Kauffman, Stuart. 1995. *At Home in the Universe*. New York, Oxford: Oxford Univ. Press.

Raff, Rudolf A. 1996. *The Shape of Life, Genes, Development, and Evolution of Animal Form*. Chicago and London: Univ. of Chicago Press.

Rasmussen, Steen, Kiaohai Chen, David Deamer, David Krakauer, Norman Packard, Mark Stadler, and Mark Bedau. 2004. "Transitions from Nonliving to Living Matter." *Science* 303: 963-65.

Ridley, Matt. 1992. "Swallows and Scorpionflies Find Symmetry is Beautiful." *Science* 257: 327-28.

Runnegar, Brenda. 1994. "Proterozoic fossils of soft-bodied metazoan (Ediacara faunas)." In *The Early Life on Earth*, ed. S. Bengston, 369-88. New York: Columbia Univ. Press.

Russell, Robert J. 1993. "Introduction." In *Quantum Cosmology and the Laws of Nature: Scientific Perspectives on Divine Action*, ed. Robert J. Russell, Nancey Murphy, and C. J. Isham, 1-32. Vatican City State: Vatican Observatory Publications, and Notre Dame, Ind.: Univ. of Notre Dame Press.

Schaff, Philip. [1910] 1919. *Creeds of Christendom, with a History and Critical Notes*. Vol. 1: *The History of Creeds*. New York and London: Harper and Brothers.

Seife, Charles. 2003. "Illuminating the Dark Universe." *Science* 302: 2038-39.

Witten, Charles. 2005. "Unraveling String Theory." *Nature* 438: 1085-87.

Zamore, Philip, and Benjamin Haley. 2005. "Ribo-gnome: The Big World of Small RNAs." *Science* 309: 1519-24.

In memory of Hans Urs Cardinal von Balthasar

CAN GOD BE GOD IN THAT WHICH IS NOT GOD? ATTEMPT AT A CHRISTOLOGY-CENTERED VIEW OF CREATION.

> God is love, and all his operations proceed from love. Once he wills to manifest that goodness by sharing his love outside himself, then the Incarnation becomes the supreme manifestation of his goodness and love and glory.
>
> —*St. Lawrence of Brindisi*

Christmas and Creation: Are both rooted in God's logic of incarnation?

OVERVIEW

There are serious current problems between the scientific understanding of cosmogenesis and the perspective from Christianity on creation. Although the models of cosmogenesis that science constructs are by no means complete, there are insights into cosmogenesis that will not change anymore. One of these most basic discoveries of science is that the cosmos has a history. The way it is now is the result of long process, one that begun in an original explosion some 14 billion years ago. In addition to the discovery of this original event, science has also gained significant insights into this creative process that brought forth atoms, stars, galaxies, planetary systems, life, increasingly complex organisms, including us. At the center of this scientific understanding of cosmogenesis is the notion that nature brought forth all that is by natural means, not by any type of design or other supernatural intervention(s).

From the view of some religions this basic tenet of science is dubbed "materialism.'" This because there is seemingly no spiritual principle involved in this scientific understanding of cosmogenesis. At the bottom of this controversy lurks the old philosophical problem of how matter may or may not relate to spirit and mind. Christianity, for example, holds that only God creates, and that all of creation is his work. From this perspective therefore, the claim from science that nature brought forth all that is, can be nothing else but atheism.

Given these mutually exclusive positions, of scientific cosmogenesis on one side and Christianity on the other, it seems hopeless to even think about trying to build a bridge over this gaping abyss. Yet, the construction of such a bridge between Christianity and science is precisely the purpose of this writing. The effort is based on the conviction that there must be one Truth; that Christian revelation about the origin of creation cannot contradict what science discovered about how the world came into existence. From this perspective there must be a unifying principle, a synthesis in which these mutually exclusive views are respected but reconciled. Such a synthesis, however, cannot be constructed by absorbing either view into its opposing position. Rather, the synthesis to be searched for must unify these two opposing positions into an oneness that not only respects but also affirms their difference. In addition, the construction of such a bridge cannot be built on sand, but must be anchored in bedrock on both sides. On the side of science this secure ground is that nature is capable of constructing itself.

Searching for this bedrock on the Christian side of the ravine one must ask the question: "What is the central revelation to Christian faith, what is the most fundamental dogma of Christianity? The answer from the Church to this question is unwavering, clear, and straightforward: *"Deus caritas est,"*[1] God is love!

Given these two solid grounds we must now assemble the parts from which to construct the bridge. In Part I, I suggest to get some elements from Christianity. In part II, I shall attempt to gather construction elements on the other side of the abyss, on the side of science. The rationale is to then join the two legs assembled from either side to complete the arch over the rift.

Part III briefly describes two current religious perspectives on cosmogenesis, and Part IV sketches an updated Christian theology of nature.

---

[1]   Encyclical Letter *Deus Caritas Est* Of The Supreme Pontiff Benedict XVI, To The Bishops, Priests And Deacons, Men And Women Religious,And All The Lay Faithful On Christian Love. Given in Rome, at Saint Peter's, on 25 December, the Solemnity of the Nativity of the Lord, in the year 2005, the first of my Pontificate.

Part I: Elements from Christianity

Christians know from Holy Scripture that God creates the world. God speaks and creation becomes! It is the Word of God that creates (Gn. 1). The prophet Isaiah adds an important dimension to this revelation. He writes: "For just as rain and snow fall from heaven and do not return there without saturating the earth and making it germinate and sprout, and providing seed to sow and food to eat, so my Word that comes from my mouth will not return to me empty, but it will accomplish what I please, and will prosper in what I send it [to do]" (Isaiah 55:10-11).

The Word of God, therefore, is not just a vibration of air. Rather, it executes the will of the one who speaks. It will saturate the Earth with rain and snow to make it germinate and sprout.

How can a word do that? How can a word accomplish a mission, how can it accomplish the task that God sends it to do? The answer to this question comes later in the history of revelations. It can be found in the New Testament, where the Gospel of John begins this way: "In the beginning was the Word, and the Word was with God and the Word was God (Jn 1:1).

The first half of this sentence confirms what we already knew from the Genesis text, namely that creation is created through the Word of God. The second part of John's sentence, however, that "the Word was with God and the Word *was* God" is crystal clear yet perplexing. It is perplexing because God and the Word that he speaks is the same, namely God, yet different. There is God and there is also the expression of God, his Word. This expression of God is God's perfect utterance, perfect because this expression of God is also God. We must therefore conclude that there is difference *within* God. There is God and there is his perfect expression, his Word that is also God.

We are here at a central revelation to Christian faith. The magisterium of the Church formulates this understanding of Christian faith this way: *"The divine persons are really distinct form one another.* God is one but not solitary. 'Father, 'Son,' 'Holy Spirit' are not simply names designating modalities of divine being, for they are really distinct from one another: 'He is not Father who is the Son, nor is the Son he who is the Father, nor is the Holy Spirit he who is the Father or the Son.' They are distinct from one another in their relations of origin: 'It is the Father who generates, the Son who is begotten, and the Holy Spirit who proceeds.' The Unity is Triune."[2]

---

2   Catechism of the Catholic Church: # 254. Doubleday, New York 1994.

The revelation in John's prologue uncovers a dimension of the Word of God that is again astounding. It states that through this Word of God that is God, namely the Son of God, "all things came to be through him, and without him nothing came to be" (Jn. 1:3).

The text again is crystal clear but illogical: How can the word of God *that is* God bring forth creation *that which is not* God? Our mind refuses to accept such a self-contradicting statement. This because our logic insists that something cannot be that which it is not! Yet this paradox that God can be God in that which is not God, is precisely the content of John's second sentence. The prologue to his gospel also sheds a light into the depth of what we already heard form Isaiah. It is that "(the) Word that comes from my mouth will not return to me empty, but it will accomplish what I please, and will prosper in what I send it [to do]." John's prologue illuminates Isaiah's text. In its light one can see that this departure of the Word of God is not just an increase in distance but is an essential transformation. God eternal departs from God to become that, which is not God but created existence, that which must become in time, the otherness of eternity. God the Son, the "otherness" of God within God, departs into creation, the otherness of God outside of God, as Hegel puts it.[5] This is not philosophical sophistry but incarnation theology: "For from him and through him and for him are all things" (Rom 11:36). "For in him were created all things . . ." (Col 1:16; "(God) spoke to us through a son . . . through whom he created all things" (Heb 1: 2); "(Jesus Christ) through whom all things are and through whom we exist" (Cor 8: 6).

Must we not conclude from these solemn statements about creation that the Word of God that is God is not absorbed into creation but remains to be God? But how so? There is no logical answer to this question. There is no way arround this paradox of Christian faith that almighty God can be God in that, which is not God! Yet this paradox is at the center of Christianity because it is the paradox of incarnation!

The mystery of incarnation; three voices from the past: Maximus the Confessor, John Scottus Eriugena, and Saint Bonaventure

Maximus was the one who experienced the mystery of the hidden Word of God in the wonders of creation most intensely. Hans Urs von Balthasar writes:

---

[3]   G. Hegel, *Philosophy of Nature.* Ed. and trans. M. J. Petry. (London: Humanities Press, [1872] 1970), 206.

"Maximus can be considered the most world-affirming thinker of all the Greek Fathers; his basically positive attitude toward nature goes even beyond Gregory of Nyssa. While Origen considers Scripture as alone supremely normative, Maximus accepts also the natural world, contemplated in the light of revelation, as a source of wisdom. Perfect knowledge—the knowledge of the believing Christian and even the knowledge of the mystic—is gleaned from both 'books' together."[4] "The wise person stands in the midst of the world's realities as in an inexhaustible treasure of knowledge. No being leaves him untouched; everything provides food for his intellectual nourishment."[5] Why does Maximus point to the book of nature? Because it is also in creation, not in the Bible alone that God reveals himself.

John Scottus Eriugena writes: "For everything that is understood and sensed is nothing but the apparitions of what is not apparent, the manifestation of the hidden, the affirmation of the negated, the comprehension of the incomprehensible [the utterance of the unutterable, the access to the inaccessible], the understanding of the unintelligible, the body of the bodiless, the essence of the superessential, the from of the formless, the measure of the measureless, the number of the unnumbered, the weight of the weightless, the materialization of the spiritual, the visibility of the invisible.[6]

What is the root of such unwavering dialectic? It is the mystery of incarnation, the mystery that almighty God can become that which is not God but a human being. Incarnation is the center of Christian faith. From this center shines a light that illuminates not only Christmas but also creation. Christmas and creation have their root in the Word of God. Both events are rooted in the eternal decision of God to give his Word away to creation.

Saint Bonaventure writes about this gift: "If, therefore, the Father bestows the Son upon the world, then he gives it along with him (the Son) everything that he was, everything that he possessed, everything that he could."[7]

---

4   Hans Urs Cardinal von Balthasar, *Cosmic Liturgy. The Universe According to Maximus the Confessor.* Translate by Brian E. Daley, S.J. (A Communio Book, San Francisco: Ignatius Press, 2003), 61.

5   bid., 62.

6   John Scottus Eriugena's *Periphyseon: On the Division of Nature* P.III 633 A, 678C. Cited in: Deirdre Carabine: *Great Medieval Thinkers: John Scottus Eriugena.* (Oxford University Press, 2000), 49.

     To here also belongs Luther's formula of "Deus absconditus sub contrario."

7   Cited from H. U. Cardinal von Balthasar: *The Glory of the Lord; a Theological Aesthetics."* Vol. II: *"Studies in Theological Styles."* (San Francisco: Ignatius Press,1984), 292.

Maximus the confessor insists that the Bible and the book of nature reveal God (Galileo comes to mind). Scottus Eriugena unfolds the dialectic of incarnation that God can be God in that, which is not God; and Saint Bonaventure is at awe about the generosity of God, astounded about his sacred gift, given away to the world. Incarnation is the event in which this gift becomes reality for the world. Through Incarnation the world becomes. Through incarnation of the Word of God that is God, creation, that which is not God, comes into existence. Thanks to this Word incarnate, this gift of God to creation, creation is capable of becoming itself. God is love; *Deus caritas est.* The love of God is the source of this gift. The gift is his Word given away to the creation. This is why nature is creative, capable of freely becoming *itself!* Therefore, cosmogenesis is not a result of mechanistic deistic teleology, not a consequence of supernatural (theistic) guidance, not a result of intelligent design but becomes freely through its own natural laws. This is precisely what science finds. What is the link from science to natural philosophy and natural theology? It is that the center of creation, the nature of nature, is the creative Word of God given away to creation.

This gift of the Word of God to creation still has another essential dimension. It is that through this gift creation is not only created in Christ but also saved. For us who are in time, creation is before salvation. Salvation is through Christ's saving death and resurrection. The birth of Christ in the Christmas event is a reality in the history of creation. Yet for God the incarnation of his Word is a reality anchored in his eternity. For God eternal, past, present, and future, are one. This is why the incarnation of his Word, namely the coming of Christ into time, is also the coming of eternity into time. With the Incarnation of the eternal Word of God into time, eternity crosses time for all time. [8] Therefore, the incarnation of the eternal Word of God in the event of Christmas is an event that unifies all time, past present, and future. Through the incarnation of the eternal Word of God in the Christmas event, time is taken up into eternity yet without destroying time. This is because in Christ, God and creation are totally different but one.

Part II: Cosmogenesis, the view from science

The new world-view from science recognizes that we live in an emergent universe. This view on cosmogenesis was prepared and supported by quite

---

8   This is paraphrasing a sentence by H. U. Cardinal von Balthasar, in: *"Theologie der Geschichte."* (Einsiedeln: Johannes Verlag, 1959), 69.

a few scientists/philosophers of the 19th and 20ies century. Among them were the philosopher/psychologist Christian von Ehrenfels (1859-1932), the experimental psychologist J. M. Baldwin (1861-1934), the geneticist/ embryologist C. L. Morgan (1852-1936), the psychologist W. Köhler (1887-1967), and the scientist/philosopher K. Popper (1902-1994).[9] I share their view that synthesis brings forth new emergent entities. This in the sense that "emergent entities are both real and causally efficacious."[10]

Emergence is the result of synthesis, it is the phenomenon that synthesis brings forth novelty with qualities that the parts that were unified do not have. Each unifying event brings forth emergent novelty. The energy released in the Big Bang is driving the process. The first force-carrying particle(s) froze out from a part of this tremendous energy. Cooling of the initial plasma lead to the formation of the first atoms. Then increasingly complex atoms emerged, and still emerge, through synthesis in the nuclear furnaces of the stars. Over hundreds of millions of years some stars explode and spew their contents into interstellar space. Clouds form in this way that through gravitational collapse crystallize into planetary systems.[11] Similar to probably countless other planetary systems in the universe, our solar system came also into existence in this way.

On Earth radiation energy, including the one provided by the sun, made chemical syntheses possible. Molecular complexification produced pre-life molecules. Life emerged from their integration into information carrying, replicating living entities, capable of adapting to changing environments. The process of complexification that already occurred at the pre-life level continued at the level of organisms. We are beginning to gain an insight into how this happens. The complexification that brings forth new forms of life is most likely a consequence of complexification at the level of the organismic information. Genes are these units of information. They are capable of interacting with one another. This interaction results in hierarchically organized physiological entities. Some primary genes higher up in the hierarchy control the activity of genes at lower levels. Once they are active some of them might produce products that turn primary genes off. Genes interacting in this way form genetic networks. They control when, where,

---

[9]   K. Popper, *Unended Quest. An Intellectual Autobiography* (La Salle and London, 1982, 178-180, 190.

[10]   G. Peterson, *Species of Emergence.* (Zygon J. of Rel/Sci. 41, 2006), 700.

[11]   R. Kerr: *Planetary Systems Proliferate.* (Science 286, 1999), 65-69.

and how long genes work. The ensemble of interacting genes of an organism (the genotype) generates the genetic programs that organize the construction of organisms (the phenotype). If the genotype changes, the phenotype might change also. Obviously, a new phenotype, a new organism must be capable to survive and produce offspring. If it cannot, it will be eliminated. The elimination of unfit phenotypes or, alternatively, the favoring of organisms that are fit to survive in a given environment, is referred to as natural selection. The evolution of life, therefore, is a consequence of a two-step creative process: changing genotypes (mutations) and natural selection. It is (genetic) variation and survival of the fittest that drives evolution. [12] It is this Darwinian mechanism that brings forth variations (by mutations) in the individuals of a species. As a consequence the composition of species may change because changing environments favor the best-adapted individuals to multiply. Over time these replace those individuals that are less fit to produce offspring.

Among many insights into how life evolves gained since Darwin the most important one in my view is the realization, how complicated the phenomenon of variation really is. There are a multitude of interacting causes that generate genetic variation. Among these are various types of mutations such as spontaneously changing individual genes, genes changing positions within or between chromosomes, loss of genes and/or entire chromosomes, duplications of genes and chromosomes, and even duplications of entire genomes. In addition, there is the recognition that new genes may become incorporated into already existing genomes by horizontal gene transfer, by viral infections, for example. There are uncountable numbers of different genes in the zillions of viruses in the seawater. [13] Through viral infections therefore, genomes might gain new genetic information. Genes acquired in this way might become integrated into the genetic networks of genomes. Once this happens the newly acquired genes might increase survival rates. Perhaps they may even shift the balance of a genetic network into a new genetically stable state. Such events may have significantly contributed to the emergence of new forms of life.

Another crucial insight into the evolution of genomes is that once a genetic program is assembled it might be arround for hundreds of millions of years. Genes and genetic programs that were assembled in bacteria and

---

[12]   Ch. Darwin, *The Origin of Species* 1859 (London: John Murray 1902).

[13]   N. Goldenfeld and C. Woese, *Biology's next revolution*. (Nature 445, 2007), 369.

unicellular organisms, way back in evolution, are still a part of modern forms of life including us![14]

A new view from science is therefore that at all levels of nature complexity may increase. This not only at the physical level of the universe but from the original explosion to atoms, molecules, to life, and all forms of organisms and us. The new view is that there is one process that brought forth everything. The process is creative by unifying elements that it already brought forth. Unification brings forth emergent novelty. From this perspective the universe is the result of one, and only one, natural, creative process.

Part III: Two religious perspectives on nature: Pantheism and Panentheism

Most scientists I know fiercely defend the capacity of nature to bring forth all that is by natural means, not by supernatural intervention(s). For example the mathematician, biologist, philosopher, Stuart Kauffman writes about creation: "In my mind and heart, the overwhelming answer is that the truth, as best as we know it, that all arose with no Creator agent, all on its wondrous own, is so awesome and stunning that it is God enough for me and I hope much of mankind. Thus, beyond the new science that glimmers a new world-view, we have a new view of God, not transcendent, not an agent, but as the very creativity in the universe itself."[15]

Stuart Kauffman proposes an answer here that many scientists will support. Is this atheism? If it is, then many scientists are indeed non-believers. They don't want to hear about a creator God that interferes in nature by either direct creative acts or by design. Why not? Because there is no evidence! The astonishing evidence is that nature brings forth novelty not by supernatural interference nor by "intelligent design" but by creative tinkering. In addition, scientists mistrust most masters of religions because they have a tendency to think that they already know everything. So why update a perspective on creation if there is nothing to revise on the old points of view? It is a matter of fact therefore, that with rare exceptions, religious leaders have no interest in the discoveries of science. Scientists instead, by there profession, have to

---

[14]   B. Ellis, *A view from the Genome.* (http://pr.caltech.edu/periodicals/EandS/ articles/evolution.pdf). E. Pennisi, *Genomicists Tackle the Primate Tree.* (Science 316, 2007), 218-221.

[15]   S. Kauffman, *Beyond Reductionism: Reinventing the Sacred.* (Zygon, J. Rel. Sci. 42), 903-914.

be open for the new, the unexpected. In addition, they are fascinated about how nature works. That is why they invest their life. They have their noses right on the wondrous complexity of nature and are at awe about how these marvels could come into existence. This wondering about the miracles of nature however, must sooner or later lead scientists to one really fundamental question: "Why is there anything at all rather than nothing?"

It is intriguing to me that Ursula Goodenough asks this basic question (p. 167) but gives no answer. Stuart Kauffman's view that "as best as we know it, that all arose with no Creator agent" violates an axiom. It is self-evident to our mind that all effects must have a cause. Therefore, nature cannot be its own cause to come into existence. There must be a creator that brought forth all that is. The question of course is: how? Is there a possibility to help finding an answer from a Christian point of view?

I think that Christianity can very well understand why pantheism, the view that nature *is* God, is so plausible and attractive to scientists. After all Christianity knows from revelation that creation is created through the Word of God that *is* God! There are many scientists who have a keen sense for the holy in nature. They are precisely right: nature *is* holy. Why? Because at the center of nature at its depth, there is the Word of God that is God! "How so?" There is this central paradox in Christianity that says that God can be God in that which is not God. It is the paradox of incarnation the illogicality that God can be God in that, which is not God. Pantheism reduces this paradox to pious atheism because if nature *is* God then there is no personal God that transcends nature.

The attempt to resolve the Christian paradox of incarnation by warping it to conform to human logic leads to another inadequate view of the Christian paradox of incarnation the various models of panentheism. Its approach to rationalize how God interacts with the world tries to resolve the mystery of incarnation by splitting God into a temporal and an eternal pole. In this model God transcends creation but is also immanent in creation. He is immanent in creation in such away that creation becomes God's project through which God completes himself.[16]

That God must complete himself through bringing forth creation contradicts, however, the traditional Christian understanding that God creates creation freely, not out of necessity to construct himself. God is not

---

16   Ch. Hartshorne, *A Natural Theology for Our Time*. (Morse Lectures, La Salle, Publishing Co. 1964), 126-137.

dependent on time to complete himself because for God eternal past, present, and future are one![17]

Other panentheistic models of how God interacts with the world suggest that the world is in "some sense 'in God,' but of God as 'being more than' the world, and so as the circumambient Reality in which the world persists and exists ('pan-en-theism).[18] In this model the mind-body analogy is used to explain that God acts on creation similar to how our mind interacts with the body. [19] I have great respect for the efforts made by the thinkers that suggest panentheistic models of how God interacts with the world. In my view, however, these models do not fully respect God's free action to create on one hand and the freedom of creation to become itself on the other. As I see it, freedom on both sides is a fundamental prerequisite for the Christian revelation that God is love. This is because without freedom, there cannot be a loving relationship. Yet at the heart of Christianity is the invitation of God to enter into such a loving relationship. This offer is made through Christ. He is the gift of God to creation so that God and creation be one. "For God so loved the world that he gave his one and only Son, . . . (Jo 3:16).

This gift of God to the world is his creative Word through which all of creation is created. It is the Son of God that is God, yet given away to creation so that creation, not God again, may become. This gift of God to the world is a true gift, a gift really given away, not a grant! A grant is not really given away because a grant has conditions, strings attached to it. In contrast, a gift is unconditional, truly given away so that the receiver can really receive it. Receiving a gift is really only received if it now belongs to the one who received the gift and therefore now possesses it. The point is that the gift of the Word of God to creation now belongs to creation. Creation can do with this gift whatever it pleases for the gift is really received. From this it follows that the center of nature, the creative core of nature, is the Word of God that is God, yet given away to the otherness of God, creation! It is thanks to this gift that creation is capable of becoming itself. Because the nature of nature is the Word of God in the otherness of creation, the scientific discoveries about nature are of deep and essential relevance to Christian theology. This is because Christians know from old that the glory of

---

[17]   K. Barth, *Church* Dogmatics. Vol. II: *The Doctrine of God*. (Edinburgh, T. and T. Clark, 1975), 608-640.

[18]   A. Peacock, *Theology for a Scientific Age, Being and Becoming- Natural, Divine, and Human*. (Minneapolis MN, Fortress Press, 1993), 158.

[19]   Ibid., 161.

God can be seen in all that is. "The heavens declare the glory of your hands" (Ps 19:1); and "I saw the glory of the God of Israel coming from the east. His voice was like the roar of rushing waters, and the land was radiant with his glory" (Eze 43:2); "Heaven and Erath are full of your glory" (Mass, Gloria"). As I have briefly described above, many scientists experience this glory of God in nature but there is the pantheistic tendency towards dissolving God in nature. Why do some of them hold such pantheistic shaded belief? Most likely because their scientific research provides them with actual insights into the wonder of the particular phenomena of nature they explore.

Scientists construct models of nature. Doing so they explore the wonders of creation by investing their life. What other seal of authenticity could there be? Although it is illegitimate to claim the truth uncovered by science to be the only truth, it is also impossible to remain a credible witness to the truth of Christianity by ignoring the discoveries of science. This because the truth discovered by the methods of science must be an essential dimension of the truth that Christianity proclaims. Why? "Because God is the source of all Truth. His Word in Holy Scripture and in creation *is* truth;"[20]

The New Testament reveals that God created everything by the eternal Word, his beloved Son. In him 'all things were created, in heaven and on earth . . . all things were created through him and for him.'"[21] From the Christian point of view, science is theology because science is deeply involved in studying God as he reveals himself through his Word in creation. There is the theology based on the revelation of the Word of God in Holy Scripture; but there is also the theology based on the revelation of the Word of God in creation. The Church therefore has a deep reason to carefully consider the scientific models of cosmogenesis. A rift between the theology based on Holy Scripture and the theology based on the book of nature is impossible; one Galileo affair is already one too many! The question of course is how to integrate the insights from modern science into Christianity. What follows is perhaps a first step toward this goal.

Part IV: Sketching a Christian theology of nature for our time

Scientists have no choice; they must insist that nature constructs itself. Why? Because there is solid evidence that nature brought forth all that is through a

---

[20]   *Catechism of the Catholic Church*, (New York, Doubleday, 1995), #215, # 2465.
[21]   Ibid., #291, # 241.

natural historical (probabilistic) sequence of syntheses. This natural sequence of syntheses can therefore not be deterministic, goal-oriented. Complexity increases by natural means. It does so through the integration of that which was already previously integrated. Therefore the hallmark of cosmogenesis is that everything that is, exists as unity. Unities, however, are not flat simplicities in the sense that they contain all the same elements. Rather, unites are always complex because their oneness emerges from the integration of diversity. Synthesis therefore brings forth new unities that are "simply" one, but as a consequence of integrating diversity, all true unity is complex. This is the reason why all that exists is unified diversity, "simple" complexity. This is also the why the ontological structure of all that exists is *simplex*.

Teilhard de Chardin

That synthesis is creative is also one of the central themes of Father Teilhard de Chardin's work.[22] He pointed out that synthesis brought forth successive levels of emergent complexity from mater to the noosphere, the level of human thought. I share his view that synthesis brings forth new levels of reality, that cosmogenesis is the result of sequential unification. However, I must disagree with Teilhard's view that the process of complexification is goal-oriented. I must disagree because one fundamental insight from modern science is that the process of cosmogenesis is deeply probabilistic. This is to say that cosmogenesis is a genuine historical process. What happens occurs within a field of also possible events; which one really happens opens a new set of possible events, and so on. Because of this essentially probabilistic nature of the creative process there cannot be a predetermined goal at the beginning of the process. Nature is not an organism that develops into an adult in a predictable way. Organisms can do that because there is a (genetic) program that guides the process; the process, however, that brings forth the universe has no such program! In other words, there is teleology in organismic development but not in cosmogenesis. Nature is creative through a historical (probabilistic) sequence of syntheses. It is by creative through inventive tinkering not by any kind of supernatural intervention, including design. This is to say that, *nature is free to become itself!*

This poses a serious problem for the Christian notion of providence. How can God's plan for creation become reality if creation is capable of freely constructing itself?

---

22   P. Teilhard de Chardin, *The Phenomenon of Man*. (New York, Harper and Row 1959).

The history of creation and the history of salvation

This is an essential issue for the relationship between the history of creation and the history of salvation. How may it be possible to find a solution to this problem respecting both a scientific world-view and the perspective from Christianity?

The incarnation of the eternal Word of God in the Christmas event crosses time for all time. Therefore, salvation is not an event to be expected sometime in the future but is always now. Salvation through the sacrifice of Jesus Christ dying on the cross is salvation for all time, past, present, and future. The cross therefore is the center of salvation for all history, cosmic and human. It is the center around which the history of the world is revolving: "Stat crux dum orbitur orbis!"[23] Therefore, the history of the world does not run parallel to the history of salvation. The history of the world is not oriented towards a point in the future in which God and creation will be reconciled. Rather, Christ dying on the cross has reconciled God and the world for all time.

It seems to me that Christianity requires creation to be free to become itself. From the Christian perspective, human beings are the representatives of creation for "creation waits in eager expectation for the sons of God to be revealed" (Ro 8: 19). And how is it that human beings may become sons of God? It is by being open to accept the loving relation ship offered by God to his children. And this is the deep reason why nature and human beings have to be free: It is that love cannot be imposed. The commitment necessary in any loving relationship can only be entered freely. Freedom of God and freedom of creation are two foundational preconditions for Christianity to make sense. Why? Because God is love!

If we ponder this statement from the fundamental dogma of Christianity that God is love, then it becomes quite clear why it is that nature is free to become itself. Basically this view from science is implied in the Christianity revelation that God is love. It is implied because a loving relationship is impossible without freedom. Freedom is the prerequisite for making the decision to either accept of reject it. Therefore freedom of God to create and freedom of nature to become itself are essential dimensions of the fundamental dogma of Christianity that God is love. Thanks to this freedom given by

---

[23]   Carthusian inscription on the bottom of a stone cross: Church yard, San Angel, Mexico City.

God through the present of his Word, nature is capable of bringing forth a creature that is free. Free to discover that creation is God's gift, and perhaps give thanks through gratefully living one's life.

Reflecting about the nature of giving we found that a true gift is giving away of oneself. God gave away himself to creation before the world begun. And when the time was right, that which had happened before the world begun became visible. It became visible in the Christmas event, the event in which God became Man. In this event God showed his almighty power, the power that he can become that witch he is not: a Man! Incarnation! What a mystery! God becoming that which God is not, a human being! There is no way human logic can resolve this paradox, yet is at the center of Christian faith.

Pope John Paul II addressing the Bishops of the Catholic Church writes: "The mystery of the Incarnation will always remain the central point of reference for an understanding of the enigma of human existence, the created world and God himself. The challenge of this mystery pushes philosophy to its limits, as reason is summoned to make its own a logic which brings down the walls within which it risks being confined."[24]

Yes, incarnation happened at Bethlehem in the land of Judah some two thousand years ago. That event happened when the time was right. It was right because God's people had finally learned that he is a caring, loving God. And so the time was right, for there was Mary, full of grace, ready, open, to receive the Word of God that is God to become a human being, that which certainly is not God! What happened, however, at the first Christmas made visible what is invisible, namely that the Word of God, that was with God before creation, created creation, namely that which is *essentially* not God. Christmas shows that God almighty can be God in that which is not God. Incarnation out of which creation came into existence at the beginning of time came within the history of creation at Bethlehem, in the land of Judah! Christmas and creation are therefore both anchored in God's logic of incarnation. God's eternal decision of incarnation, to give away his creative Word, is the center of creation and salvation. "In all wisdom and insight, he has made known to us the mystery of his will in accord with his favor that he set forth in him as a plan for the fullness of times, to sum up all things in Christ, in heaven and on earth" (Eph 1: 7-10).

---

[24] John Paul II, *Fides et Ratio*, letter to the Catholic Bishops, (1998), #84.

Conclusion

The fundamental discovery by modern science is that nature is capable of bringing forth itself. It is the prerequisite for bringing forth a creature that is free. That God is love is the fundamental dogma of Christianity. Any loving relationship is based on freely deciding whether to enter the bondage of love. Therefore, what science discovered is only making explicit what is already implied in the Christian revelation that God is love.

INDEX